for Pat Patrick
who visited Pleasant Valley
several times while he was
part of the Riley family.

J. Riley Helmstetter

Feb. 16, 1998

a gift
from your daughter —
and my niece —
Anne Maureen
Ines

And the Coyotes Howled

Family Adventures in Pleasant Valley

I. Riley Helmstetter

BookPartners, Inc.
Wilsonville, Oregon

BookPartners, Inc.
P.O. Box 922
Wilsonville, Oregon 97070

Dedication

In memory of my parents, Bill and Audrey Riley. Their tough love taught self-reliance, which provided unique adventures and left me this inheritance of memories. For my children, Doug, Janet Eileen, and Curt.

Bill Riley with dead bear.
1943

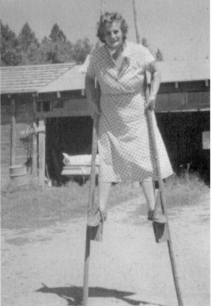

Audrey Riley on stilts.
Mom liked to join in
our fun. 1955

Riley kids December 1941:
Dora, Lester, Ines, Leola,
Viola, Vida, Effie.

Acknowledgments

This book is all Jeaninne Helmstetter's fault. She pestered me until I put in writing the stories I had been telling her daughter, Deidre, who was growing up in Japan. Immersed in a far different culture, this granddaughter was hungry for "pioneer" tales of rural America.

No different than in my childhood, I'm still relying on family. Sisters Kit (Dora), Leola and Effie, and brother Lester filled in gaps and jarred my memory, opening doors to moments long forgotten. Lester's son, Tony, set me straight on logging terminology. Uncle Lester Steeley told stories about Mom and Dad's early married life. And my daughter's husband, David Kyle, spent many hours transferring my typing to a computer disk.

At a faltering early stage, Pat Davis, Margaret and Don Trowbridge, Jane Ellis, Ruth Lovelady, Opal and Dewey Powell, Liz Lieberman, Dottie and Ray Metter prodded me into going on.

Significant data and private pictures came from Rose Aubertin Geer, Jo and Louis Nullett, Ernie and Pat McKinney, Ethel Holter, Letha Peters, Ralph Byrd, Alvin Conner, Barbara Loven Scott, Dee and Ina McKern, Belva and Bob Riddle, George and Lydia Cranston, Howard Esvelt, Ruth Heidegger McNutt, Margaret Heidegger Paladeni, Jean Heidegger Pauley, Pady Rose, George Lucero, Mick Johnson, Goldie Entwistle and her children, Gerry Fredrickson, Janice Harlick and Bill Entwistle.

Adra Chamberlin took me over the hills of her (Rupert's) farm to the Curry Place to find traces of our old trail.

Drawing a picture of a sack-sewer's needle, former wheat rancher Ray Hunt described Dad's job as a sack sewer during wheat harvest, and reminded me of that terminology.

My writing-critique group forced me to go into depth to bring the past to life, and helped me find the right voice. I would not have finished had it not been for Raven Parris, Laura Underwood, Cathey Daniels, Becky Bolinger, Kay Brookshire, Russ Manning, Lavon Crews and Patrick Killeen.

In the final stage, Jennifer Jordan-Henley, writing specialist at Roane State Community College, Oak Ridge Campus, spurred me on to completion with her enthusiasm and optimism.

While I sifted through more than sixty years of memories, my husband (understanding my compulsion to record my childhood) gave me extra writing time by becoming chief cook and bottle washer. And in hearing each new story with a critical ear, he also served as my listening post.

And much like my mother did when turning scraps of cloth into patchwork quilts, Ursula Bacon, my editor, cut and pieced my lengthy manuscript until she turned it into a book.

To all, I say, "Thank you, *gracias, domo arrigato*, and *merci*."

Author's Note

This book portrays everyday country life during the Great Depression in rural Eastern Washington.

While the various adventures are as I remember them, they may differ from memories that others have of the same time. Relatives and friends might write entirely different versions — and all would be true.

Table of Contents

Prologue
1990-1991

It was December of 1990. For the eleventh year Henry and I were spending the winter in Mexico. Tennessee winters are mild, but they're not as pleasant as the balmy days south of the border, where the sun shines every day. I had been passing a stable one morning and, wistfully recalling the hours spent on horseback while growing up in Eastern Washington, I decided to go for a ride.

Bouncing around in the Mexican saddle on a bony horse, I wished I could trade my mount for Betty, our smooth-riding sorrel mare which years ago took me to grade school. She rode like a rocking chair compared to this stiff-legged nag trotting along Lake Chapala's shoreline. I grabbed the big saddle horn to keep from falling off.

As Old Bones slowed from his bone-jarring trot to an easy walk, my thoughts wandered and I found myself taking a ride into the past.

My eyes didn't see the hills surrounding Lake Chapala, but conjured up a vision of Monumental Mountain in the Huckleberry Mountain Range of Washington, against the hills surrounding Lake Chapala.

Monumental Mountain dominated my view for most of my childhood in Pleasant Valley. Though not nearly as high or imposing, remembering the mountain made me think of the Andes of South America, pictured in my seventh-grade geography book. The picture that had intrigued me the most was captioned: "Lake Titicaca, the highest navigable lake in the world."

I had studied the pictures voraciously, wishing I could see those places. The geography book didn't convey what the people were like in those faraway lands, nor did they explain how folks there dressed and talked. I was more curious about the people than in learning dull statistics.

The only person I'd ever seen from another country was Chinaman Tai, the little man who sold firecrackers at our Fourth-of-July celebrations at the Quillisascut Grange Hall. His English was limited, and I couldn't speak Chinese and had been too young and shy to say more than "Two packages of firecrackers, please."

The few magazines at home didn't tell much about people in faraway lands, either. Every spare moment between chores, I read one of those magazines or books that had been passed on to us. Whenever Mom needed me, she knew she'd find me with my nose in a book.

Stories about bullfights in Spain, Western tales in *Ranch Romances* and *Western Story* magazines entranced me with all their Spanish words. My tongue formed unfamiliar words like *adios amigo, señor, señora,* and *hasta luego.* Though these stories held me spellbound, they didn't satisfy my curiosity. During the Depression — and my barefoot childhood — I never imagined I'd get to see faraway places. But years later, my husband took me to several foreign countries. In Linares, Spain, we parked beside a bull ring. Its high stone wall had a tile plaque dedicating it to their native son, Manolete, the famous bullfighter of my stories.

In Morocco, sitting beside the driver of a horse taxi, I held the reins and drove the carriage down the main avenue of Marrakesh. In Peru, I rode in a reed boat on Lake Titicaca, gazed at the Inca stronghold of Machu Picchu, and dickered in Spanish through an open train window with a Peruvian woman in her full skirt, shawl and brown bowler hat for some of her handiwork.

In Japan, after reclaiming my lost passport, I got "thrown out" of a police station. At a crafts fair in Yugoslavia when a seller didn't speak English, I was delighted to learn he spoke Spanish. Finding a common language was like finding a friend. In Egypt, a teenager in a loose aba rowed three of us across the Nile, and I silently wondered what caused the sudden bulge in front of the young man's clothing. (Gray-haired women couldn't have brought that on!) And in Turkey, our bus driver pointed to the protective blue glass "Evil Eye Protector" over the windshield as he drove the wrong way down a busy street.

It's little wonder that faraway places and their people fascinate me.

⟨⟩ ⟨⟩

After our winter in Mexico, Henry and I crossed the high desert plains between Zacatecas and Saltillo, heading home. For the past hundred miles we saw nothing more interesting than sparse forests of Joshua trees and the distant granite peaks of the Sierra Madre Oriental Mountains. Then, on the dusty tracks of a railroad siding, several boxcars stood motionless under the hot sun. Bright flowers bloomed in tin cans nailed to their wooden sides, and newly washed clothes sprawled over nearby bushes to dry.

A glimpse of these crude homes took me back many years to a logging camp and to the railroad boxcar that was once home to me. And my mind wandered, just as it had when I rode Old Bones along the lakeshore. My thoughts went back my mother's stories of her early life and on into memories of my childhood on the farm, to another world a long time ago.

Part I
1920-1929

Idaho, Oregon and Washington

1

Beginnings

It was the summer of 1920. The land lay sweltering under a hot afternoon sun that rose high in the clear, blue Idaho sky. That's where it all began.

Strange as it may seem, a bucket of water at the sheepherders' picnic broke the ice and helped Bill Riley get acquainted with Audrey Steeley. If the annual event hadn't been held that summer in Meadows, Idaho, my parents probably would never have gotten married. The two young people had lived in the same general area for about a year but had seen each other only a few times.

The sheepherders' picnic always drew a big crowd and was a major event for this small town and the large surrounding area. Children played noisy games, and grown-ups socialized before sitting down to eat at the long tables, where they continued their visiting. Audrey and Bill — both shy and reserved — had been sneaking peeks at each other ever since their initial greeting that day. Bill wanted to talk to Audrey but felt tongue-tied and ill at ease. He knew the girl's brother, Lester; and on the few occasions he had visited him had been too bashful to say much to Audrey. Without Lester at the picnic, Bill didn't know how to strike up a conversation.

The young man kept eyeing Audrey, and finally, while she was eating lunch with her mother and small brothers, crept up behind her and dumped a bucket of water over her head. Bill had found a rather unique way to get acquainted. The surprise tactic had the desired results, and soon the two young people lost their bashfulness and found lots to talk about. Before the afternoon was over, Audrey got back at her new friend by pushing him into the creek. It was her way of showing Bill she liked him.

⟨⟩ ⟨⟩

Born on July 21, 1901, in the small town of Drain, Oregon, Bill (William Lorenzo Riley) was the second son born to Peter and Dora Wheeler Riley. Brother Frank had arrived two years earlier when the Rileys lived in Colorado.

The family moved around a great deal while Peter Riley searched for a steady job. In 1913, the family — now consisting of eight children — was living in Cambridge, Idaho. Not having a farm of his own, Peter Riley worked for farmers at whatever jobs he could get. What with eight children to raise, life wasn't easy, and there was never enough money to establish a stable home life.

In 1914, when Bill was thirteen, he left home to work with his brother Frank, herding sheep. Six years later Bill struck out on his own, working for a Mr. Gilmore, who had a sheep ranch not far from New Meadows. After a few months, Bill had enough of the lonely job of sheep herding. He had heard that a man by the name of Edward Osborne needed a hand on his cattle ranch in Meadows Valley.

Bill rode his Harley Davidson to the Osborn ranch to check on the job and was hired on the spot. Lester Steeley, a ranchhand, was about the same age as Bill, and the two young men hit it off at once and liked working together. One night Lester took Bill home with him to have supper and to meet his family — his mother, Mary Margaret Denney, and her children, seventeen-year-old Audrey and three young sons, Elmo, Frank and Bob.

Bill was quite taken with Audrey's brown eyes and sweet face framed by long, dark braids. He especially liked her thick, lustrous hair— a contrast to his own thinning black hair. At the tender age of nineteen, he already had a small bald spot on top of his head.

After having spent several lonely years away from his parents, Bill enjoyed being in the midst of family life again and was soon smitten with Audrey. And with all of them calling her "Sis," it was natural for Bill to call her that, too — when he got brave enough to talk to her at all. Feeling shy around this beautiful girl, the right words wouldn't come to him. He was only at ease when everyone was present.

One thing about his new friends surprised him. He couldn't figure out how Lester could be so tall and Audrey so short. Lester was a six-footer, but his sister was only five feet one. Standing beside the young woman made Bill feel taller than his five-foot, ten-inch height.

Audrey was born to Mary Margaret Denney Steeley and George Steeley on July 30, 1903, in Cambridge, Idaho, two years after her brother, Lester. Audrey never saw her tall father, who had deserted his family shortly before her birth. Mary Margaret Denney married again. The family moved to New Meadows, where Audrey went through the eighth grade in the town's two-story brick school house.

The new husband gave Audrey's mother four sons. He also gave her a life of grief—full of hardships and beatings. In later years, Lester said of his stepfather, "He was a mean son-of-a-bitch. He tied Mother up and beat her with a leather driving rein."

The summer Audrey turned seventeen, she spent a few weeks keeping Mrs. Gilmore company at her lonely sheep camp. When Audrey returned home looking shabby in her old worn-out coat, Lester felt sorry for her. He went out and bought her a new coat, using the money he had made fighting fires for the United States Forest Service.

It wasn't long after meeting Lester's family that Bill saw a poster announcing the annual sheepherders' picnic. When the young man discovered that Audrey would be at the picnic with her family, Bill decided to go. It took a bucket of water and a dousing in the creek to bring the two young people together. They were married the following year on September 12, 1921, in Council, Idaho.

⋙ ⋘

More than sixty years after the sheepherders' picnic, Dave Kyle (my daughter Janet Eileen's husband) delighted me with the story Mom had told him about Dad dumping the bucket of water over her head. He said Mom's brown eyes sparkled in remembrance when she told about pushing Dad into the creek.

⋙ ⋘

Since Bill's motorcycle couldn't very well accommodate the wedding party, he had to borrow a team and wagon for the twenty-five-mile trip to Council, the county seat. Audrey wouldn't go without her mother, who demanded they take young Frank along, who had not gone to school because he was sick.

After the brief and simple wedding ceremony, the little family celebrated the occasion by going to a restaurant for supper. Bill then turned the team around and headed back toward New Meadows. The fifty-mile round trip was too far to make in one day, so Bill found a good spot beside the road and made camp. The newlyweds' "bed" consisted of a pile of quilts spread out under the wagon, while the bride's mother and young Frank slept in the wagonbed above them.

Audrey remarked later it wasn't a very romantic way to spend their wedding night. She had been embarrassed that her new husband insisted on starting their married life that night.

Eventually, Bill got rid of the unreliable motorcycle and bought a secondhand Dodge. It proved to be a vast improvement over the Harley Davidson, with its leather drive belt that stretched when it got wet. In rainy weather, he spent more time pushing it than riding it.

For the next couple of years, Bill worked in various places. Together with Lester Steeley, he rented a farm in South Meadows Valley. The modest house that sat on the land was Bill and Audrey's first home. To help buy the barest necessities, the men worked in the sawmill in Meadows, in between keeping the farm going.

Bill and Lester farmed for one year as sharecroppers. The two men harvested about seventy tons of good wild hay, just right for sheep. As Lester told about it later, "This old crooked farmer wanted to buy it, and we set a fair price. Then he turned right around and sold it to a sheep man for a higher price, making a big profit from our hay."

On June 27, 1922, Audrey gave birth to her first baby, a son, in South Meadows Valley, without the help of either a doctor or a midwife. When her pains started, Bill ran all the way across the valley, wading a creek midway, to tell Audrey's mother, Mary, the baby was coming. He was panting so hard from running, he could hardly give her the message, then turned around and ran back to Audrey, taking his shortcut. Mary harnessed her horse and hitched it to the buggy, arriving in plenty of time to deliver her first grand-child, Lester Wilfred Riley.

Soon afterward, Bill, Audrey and the baby moved a short distance to McCall, where Bill worked in a sawmill for a few months. Their next move took them about eighty miles south, to a farm near Weiser, Idaho, where they were still living on March 14, 1924, when I was born. Dr. Ernest Finney drove out from town in his horse and buggy to take care of Mom. When she told Dr. Finney she hadn't thought of a name for her new baby, he said, "Well, I think 'Ines' is a pretty name."

Taking the doctor's suggestion and adding her own middle name, Mom named me Ines Lillian Riley. For the first three months of my life, I was fretful most of the time, and Mom said the only time I wasn't crying was when I was nursing. When she finally took me to Dr. Finney in Weiser, he was startled by the fact that I hadn't gained much weight. He told her to put me on the bottle and feed me a diluted mixture of Eagle Brand condensed milk. After Mom did as the doctor ordered, I started gaining weight and stopped crying all the time.

❖ ❖

Thirty years after Mom first put me on the bottle of canned milk, I was cooking something using Eagle Brand condensed milk. Licking the spoon, I recognized a familiar taste, yet couldn't remember having had it before. Puzzled, I told Mom about it the next time I saw her. She said, "I fed you condensed milk when you were a baby. It probably saved your life. You were nothing but skin and bones."

It may have been that same milk that eventually brought me my height of five feet, eight inches. By the time I was ten, I'd outgrown Mom. At fourteen, I was nearly as tall as Lester and only a couple inches shorter than Dad. Since Mom was so short and Dad wasn't tall for a man, I wondered what made me so tall and skinny. When I asked Mom, she said, "Your grandmother told me that your Grandfather Steeley was over six feet tall, and you probably take after him."

⪻⪼ ⪻⪼

Realizing there just wasn't enough money in sharecropping, Dad decided to head West. He'd heard that sawmills and lumber camps in Oregon needed workers. Since he'd had some sawmill experience and was young and strong, he knew he could handle a job of a mill hand or lumberjack. Mom wondered what Oregon would be like — she'd never been out of Idaho.

My family left Idaho and ventured into new territory.

2

Our First Homes

Our new home south of Bend, Oregon, was a tent in the middle of the woods, some distance from where other loggers lived. With Dad gone, Mom felt lonely and unprotected in the wilds with only a flimsy tent sheltering her and her two small children. She had gotten in the habit of keeping Dad's loaded pistol close by. She used it one night when Dad hadn't returned from buying supplies.

She was almost asleep when she heard heavy footsteps outside the tent. The unexpected noise in the forest's silence frightened her. The shuffling noises around the tent scared Mom. It was dark, and she was alone in the tent with three-year-old Lester and me, a one-year-old. When the footsteps continued circling the tent, she was afraid someone was going to come into the tent and attack us. In a quavering voice, she yelled, "Who's out there?" The footsteps halted suddenly, but there was no reply. The abrupt silence scared Mom almost as much as the noise had. She waited a moment. There was still no answer.

Lifting the pistol with a trembling hand, Mom pointed it in the direction she'd last heard footsteps. Her finger squeezed the trigger, and the pistol roared in the darkness.

After the loud bang, silence returned to the dark woods; there weren't any more strange noises that night. Mom thought she might have killed someone. When Dad returned, she told him all about her scare.

The next morning Dad went all around the tent checking for tracks and signs of blood, and looked through nearby bushes and trees, but didn't find a trace of anyone having been there. The only thing he found on his search was a bullet hole in the wall of the tent.

Soon after the shooting incident, we moved to the main camp of the logging operations and lived in one of the company-provided cabins. Close to other families, Mom no longer felt lonely and frightened, and the deep, dark woods became less threatening. (I still have the photograph of Lester and me standing barefoot in front of a small, unpainted cabin in the midst of tall trees.)

We moved here and there because Dad worked in several different places — from Bend to Klamath Falls, where he had a job in a sawmill for a few months. When here was no more work, we packed up and headed further south, following the rumor that logging companies were looking to hire sawyers.

Every home in the various logging camp settings was no more than a temporary shelter, often rough and makeshift. But the summer tent in the woods was the flimsiest one we had. The cabin, though rough and simple, kept us dry in rainstorms. There just weren't many "real" houses out in the woods, and we had to live in whatever shelter was available.

When Dad worked near Chiloquin, our home was a railroad boxcar. The lumber company had outfitted boxcars to serve as living quarters for the loggers' families. Our sleeping cots sat at one end, the kitchen and eating area at the other. The boxcar wasn't much better equipped for cooking than the cabin had been. When Mom needed water, Dad had to carry it inside in buckets. It wasn't any problem getting rid of the dishwater — Mom just tossed it out the door.

The boxcars stood on the siding of the railroad track, out of the way of the logging activities. One day, I fell off the top step and the shiny steel track came rushing up at me, hit me on the forehead and knocked me out cold. I was unconscious when Mom carried me up the steps and put me me on my cot. The fall on the track made a deep gash that left me with a scar on my forehead.

❧ ❧

I was only three years old, but I still remember that shiny railroad track stretching out behind our boxcar for a long, long way.

❧ ❧

From our boxcar home in the logging camp, we moved to the outskirts of Klamath Falls, where Dad worked for both the Algoma and the Pelican Bay lumber companies. It was here that our new baby sister was born on May 27, 1927. My parents named her Mary Dora Riley, after their mothers.

The addition of another baby to our family made Dad realize we needed a more permanent home than the logging camps and those other places where we had lived. Mom had just received a letter from her mother with the news that Grandma and her new husband, Charley Adams, had recently moved to a farm near the town of Rice, Washington. Among other news, she wrote, "There are farms for rent here — cheap. You might like living in Stevens County. It's a pretty country."

Mom thought living on a farm would be better for a family than living in logging camps. Dad agreed and believed farming would be a more dependable way of making a living than logging, and might even be a little easier than cutting down trees all day with a crosscut saw. My parents wanted to live in one place long enough to plant a garden and raise some of their own food; they were tired of having to buy everything from the store.

Dad finished out the logging season, got his pay, and traded in our old Dodge on a secondhand Star touring car. Painted black, it had four doors with isinglass snap-on side curtains that could be taken off in summer. In December of 1927, he loaded our few belongings into our "new" automobile, and the five of us headed north. Lester was five years old, I was three and a half, and Dora was only seven months.

Rice, our destination, was over eight hundred miles away — about forty miles south of the Canadian border. It would take us more than two weeks to get there because Dad wanted to stop in Cottage Grove, Oregon, to visit friends, and then go on to the Oregon Coast. He and Mom, curious about just how big a sight the ocean was, thought it was worth driving out of our way to see the Pacific Ocean for the first time.

We got to Cottage Grove after dark, and next morning at breakfast Dad's friend made a big impression on me. He swung me off the floor and into a high chair. I felt very big sitting up so tall. It was the first time I'd sat in a high chair.

The man's wife set a bowlful of cornflakes and sugar-coated banana slices on the tray in front of me. Cornflakes was another first for me. Breakfast at home had always been hot oatmeal or cream of wheat. After a short visit, we headed west.

We stopped at a place called Agate Beach on the coast, and

Dad rented a tourist cabin near the ocean. He set the suitcase inside, and we all ran down to the water's edge until the foaming waves covered our shoes. Looking out over the heaving waves, all we could see was more ocean until it touched the sky. Dad said, "It's big. If you could see far enough, you could see all the way to China."

We walked along the rocky beach picking up agates. When we held them up to the sun, we could see light shining through them. Some of the agates were almost clear, while others were shining black, some were red, and a few had streaks of different colors. Taking the prettiest ones to a rock shop, Dad asked if the man could polish them and was told it would take over a week to get a good polish. The shop owner had polished rocks for sale and said, "You'll enjoy them. They'll stay shiny forever."

Mom liked them so well that Dad bought as many as he could hold in both hands.

⋞⋟ ⋞⋟

The shiny agates remained special to Mom, and she kept them in a trunk with her other treasures. For years, whenever we took them out to admire their shine and feel their smoothness, we could always smell the ocean and hear the sound of the waves crashing against the shore.

⋞⋟ ⋞⋟

Several days later, when we finally got to Rice, we found it to be a very small community straddling State Highway 22 (later renumbered State Highway 25) in Stevens County, Washington. The town consisted of a post office, a general mercantile store with a gas pump out front, an IOOF Hall, and a few houses. We couldn't see the school house but learned later that there was one on the dirt road up the hill to the east. Rice sure was small. It was important only to the people there and those in the surrounding area.

Mom got out Grandma's letter from her purse and read it again for the directions to get to Pleasant Valley and the Aldredge Place, where they lived. It turned out to be up in the hills out of Rice on the Heidegger Road.

Lester watched for mailboxes alongside the road. When he spied one, Dad would slow down so he or Mom could read the names painted on the boxes. Three miles up the hill they found the one with Grandma's name on it. Dad pulled up by the wire fence in front of the house and stopped. Grandma had seen us drive up and came running out to the gate, calling excitedly, "Sis and Bill are here!"

Frank and Bob, Grandma's teenaged sons, were right on her heels to greet us. Soon all the grown-ups were laughing and talking, hugging and shaking hands. One of my uncles said to the other, "I'll carry Ines, and you can take Lester." Strong arms grabbed me as Uncle Frank lifted me out of the car and carried me into the house. At that the moment I knew our long drive from Oregon was over. I felt at home.

⋞⋟° ⋞⋟°

The town of Rice was named for William and Mary Rice, the first white settlers in the area, who had moved to Stevens County from Michigan. In 1883 the Rices bought 120 acres from an Indian named Nicolo. William, a carpenter as well as a farmer, built several houses besides the two on his property.

The first school, Columbia District, was located one-half-mile south of the village and was abandoned around 1900 when a new schoolhouse was built a short distance east of Rice on the road leading up the hill.

3

Getting Settled

We lived with Grandma and Charley on the Aldredge Place for over a month while Dad looked for a farm to rent. The small house was crammed full, what with our family of five added to their six.

Crowded as conditions were, we had to stay put until we could move into our own place and acquire a few necessary household goods. Dad settled for a farm owned by a Mr. Brady, a few miles north of Rice. Part of the land rambled down to the east bank of the Columbia River.

Our family moved to the Brady Place in late January of 1928. Dad scouted local auction sales for farm equipment and household furnishings. He didn't have enough money to buy new things and was able to stretch his meager funds by buying everything second-hand. Used things were readily available, because several farmers had given up on the land and moved away, while more prosperous farmers sold their old machinery in order to buy new ones. Buying used equipment was the cheapest way to outfit a farm, but several years later Mom mentioned she was a little tired of "buying other people's worn-out junk."

Dad bought almost everything we needed at auctions — everything from woodstoves, pots, pans, dishes, tables, chairs, fruit jars and beds for the house, to wagons, plows, a harrow, grain drill, mowing machine, rake and manure spreader for farm work. He also bought workhorses and milk cows.

Mom didn't want to drag us kids around all day, so she stayed home and let Dad do the buying. She never knew what he would bring home from the auction sales — it was always a big surprise. One day when he'd gone to a sale looking for farm equipment, he came home with something for the house instead. When he carried in the pretty kerosene lamp, I claimed it, saying it was mine. With red peonies painted on the pale green sides of its squat glass base, it was the prettiest thing I'd ever seen.

We stayed on the Brady Place just long enough for Dad to plant and harvest one crop of grain. He had to share the small income from the farm with the owner, which left him little money to feed his family. Dad needed to rent a farm that would support us, with even a few dollars left over to save up to buy a farm of his own someday. That fall he found another place to rent, and we moved again.

To get to our new home, the Meriwether Place, we had to drive down the highway toward Rice, and turn onto the Pleasant Valley Road. After topping a rise a short distance up the road, we could see Monumental Mountain looming ahead, its slopes and ridges thickly covered with pine, fir, cedar and tamarack trees. The mountain range was a beautiful sight, with its rugged summits clearly outlined against the clear blue sky. As the season changed and the first snows covered the mountain, it was even more beautiful.

The farms along the Pleasant Valley Road weren't very productive because much of the land was hilly, consisting of a light, rocky soil. In the foothills of Monumental Mountain, a farm with a hundred or more acres might have less than fifty acres level enough to plow. Some of the farmhouses were in plain sight of each other, while others were a mile and more apart.

There were only three public buildings in Pleasant Valley: the community church, the Quillisascut Grange Hall, and the two-room Pleasant Valley Grade School. The grange hall was the largest building in the valley and hosted all gatherings and social functions. In addition to the regular meetings held in the hall, there were Saturday night dances, the annual Fourth-of-July celebrations, and other community events.

Arzina Grade School sat on the winding Pleasant Valley Road about six miles from our grade school and about the same distance from the one in Rice. The only high school was in Kettle Falls, seventeen miles from home. The high school students from Arzina, Pleasant Valley, Rice, Daisy and Gifford rode the bus to Kettle Falls High School.

Soon after we moved to the Meriwether Place, I received two kinds of presents: one was a Christmas present of only slight interest to me; the other was a wonderful lesson which lasted a lifetime. Santa had left two pretty dolls in long white dresses sitting propped up on a low footstool — one for Dora and one for me.

Dora liked to play with her doll and cuddled it while sitting in the rocking chair. I admired mine but was disappointed that it couldn't do anything. Our kitty purred and snuggled, and our dog jumped up and down, wagging his tail and licking my face. All the doll could do was just sit there and look pretty. She was really kind of useless. Mom must have noticed I didn't play with it much. Neither she nor Santa ever gave me another doll.

The other present came in the form of riding lessons just before my fifth birthday. Dad, who was usually busy working, didn't spend much time with us kids, but he surprised me one afternoon. He led me to Brownie, our gentle workhorse, tied up by the barn, boosted me up on her back and handed me the reins. He showed me how to clench my knees against the horse's middle to keep my balance and told me to grab onto Brownie's mane if I started to slip off. Since I was riding bareback, there wasn't a saddle horn for hanging on, and the ground seemed a long way down. I was sure going to hang onto that mane.

My first riding lesson was so much fun that I rode every chance I got. I pestered Dad or Mom to bridle Brownie for me and help me onto her back. They didn't have to boost me up for too long; I soon learned how to make Brownie stand close to the barn so I could climb up some boards nailed to the barn and jump on her back. I didn't stray far from home, but rode around the barnyard and out into the pasture. I loved being on horseback, and it didn't matter that I couldn't go far. Brownie was a patient and steady mount and never shied or jumped around; Lester and I could ride her anytime she wasn't working in the field. We were safe; she wouldn't buck us off or run away with us.

The shortest ride I ever took was on the Meriwether Place; it lasted only about five minutes and ended up with me hopping and tiptoeing painfully through the thistles to get back to the house. I'd ridden out through the barnyard, across the little bridge over the creek, and out into the middle of the pasture. Brownie was ambling along slowly, when she spotted a good patch of grass. She stopped dead in her tracks and abruptly yanked her head down to get at the juicy-looking clump of greenery, tugging on the reins, and I went sailing over her head. I landed on the soft ground in front of her, still clutching the reins in my hands.

I wasn't hurt, but I had a different problem — I couldn't get back on the horse. I needed something to stand on, and there wasn't a block of wood or a rock in sight. I knew I was in a real predicament when I noticed a thick carpet of young bull thistles covering most of the ground around me. They were sharp and stickery — and I was barefooted!

Picking my way through the thistles, I tried to find bare ground in between those nasty, prickly things. But they grew so thick I couldn't avoid stepping on quite a few, getting stickers in my tender feet. Tears ran down my cheeks before I reached the pasture grass. I cried again as Mom picked the stickers out of the soles of my feet with a needle. Giving me a hug, she said, "I guess you've learned to steer clear of thistles now."

We lived on the Meriwether Place almost a year, when Dad heard of a farm for rent that was closer to the schoolhouse. We moved to the Hays Place just in time for Lester to start school in September 1929.

⊰⊱ ⊰⊱

Just as the seasons change the land, time brings about new happenings. The Aldredge house, where Grandma lived, has long since been torn down, and the land is now part of Terry Bolt's farm. Several years after we moved off the Meriwether Place, Sam Edwards bought it and lived there with his family.

Goldie Entwistle furnished some historical facts about Pleasant Valley. Early settlers and trappers named the area "Rat Creek Valley" (perhaps because of the abundance of muskrats), and its creek, "Quillisascut Creek," after Chief Quillisascut. Later residents changed the valley's name to "Peaceful Valley," until the day a citizen knocked a neighbor down with a monkey wrench and the man retaliated with a two-by-four. It was then renamed "Pleasant Valley" — and that's what it's still called.

Part II
1929 - 1931

The Hays Place

4

Move to the Hays Place

The farms in the lower end of Pleasant Valley had fairly level fields for farming. But going to our new home, we would be climbing into the foothills where the ground sloped up gradually from the valley, permitting some farming on hillsides that weren't too steep.

On moving day we went up the Pleasant Valley Road, which bent and curved up the center of the valley, following the creek in twists and turns. This creek came down from Monumental Mountain near Art and Ella Loven's farm and was joined by other small creeks and springs on its way down to the Columbia River.

We kept to the main road, which headed up toward the mountain. It seemed we were going to climb to the top; the farther up the road we drove, the hillier the land became. The Hays Place was not much over a mile from the Meriwether Place, but the terrain changed a good bit in that distance.

We passed Hyatts' house and then the Abernathy Place. After chugging up the hill in low gear, we arrived at our new home, which sat on top of the steep hill. Lawrence Hays, who later became one of our grade school teachers, owned the farm. At that time his house was the closest one to the top, so people just naturally got to calling the grade "the Hays Hill."

⋙ ⋘

A few years later another house was built right at the top of the hill, which was first occupied by the Raymond Heideggers, and later on by Lawrence and Ruby Hays and their two children.

⋙ ⋘

The outside of our new home looked like it had never been painted, and the boards had weathered to a dark brown. The kitchen/dining room and parlor were on the ground floor and had a small porch running across the length of it. Two bedrooms were on the second floor.

Hanging on the wall of the parlor was something I'd never seen. Mom called it a telephone. She said the strange thing would let us talk to someone way far away. One day a neighbor called us, and Mom held the receiver up to my ear so I could hear the voice coming out of it. When Mom talked, her mouth almost touched the black metal mouthpiece sticking out from the middle of the box-like instrument. But Dad soon had the telephone taken out because we couldn't afford to pay the monthly charges. He could go to a neighbor's if he needed to talk business. Anyway, few farmers had telephones in those days.

Living alongside the road with several neighbors nearby made Mom happy. She liked to visit with our closest neighbor, Mrs. Abernathy, as well Mrs. Hyatt, just a bit farther down the road. About a half-mile uphill, across from the grange hall, lived Carl and Dell Rose with their two children, Hazel and Harold. Hazel was just my age, and we soon became playmates. Her cousin, Ethel Rose, also became a good friend when her parents moved into the area.

Opal Heidegger, who had three little girls, became Mom's closest friend. Our other neighbors were the Bovee and Harris families, who lived on up the road — too long a walk for Mom to visit often.

When Lester started first grade, he had plenty of company walking to school. There was Buell Hyatt, about his age — who soon became his best friend — and his brothers. Everett Lickfold also turned into a special friend, even though he was in the seventh grade and quite a bit older. Every morning I went to the gate with Lester, but Mom wouldn't let me go any farther. After the boys walked on, I'd stand lonely at the gate, wishing I could go to school. With Lester gone all day, I was looking for a playmate, when I remembered Hazel Rose, who lived within walking distance from us.

Mom gave me permission to go to Hazel's house, and I set out walking along the edge of the graveled road. A hot September sun was beating down on the land, and the gravel under my bare feet was as hot as the stovetop. I noticed several piles of horse manure, the color of straw, all dried-up and flattened by the wheels of passing cars. I dashed from one pile to the next and stood on them for relief from the burning road.

I had worn out the previous year's shoes and was saving my new shoes for special occasions — going to town or to the grange hall. I had overheard Dad telling Mom not to spend money for unnecessary things. "If you can get along without something, don't buy it," he admonished her.

The moment I got to Hazel's house, we ran behind the grange hall and went wading in the cool, soothing waters of the creek. Hazel must have been a little lonely, too, and we had fun playing together. She let me cut out some dresses in her book of paper dolls. We put them on the dolls, folding the little tabs over the dolls' shoulders to make them stay on. Mrs. Rose treated us to slices of homebaked bread piled high with sweet raspberry jam. When my time was up, I set out for home, dreading the walk on the hot gravel. But by then the road had cooled down, and I could walk without burning my feet. From then on, Hazel and I spent a lot of time with each other, although I never had a hankering to have my own paper dolls or other toys. I'd just as soon sit on the swing, on Betty's back, or roam the outdoors, looking for adventure.

I soon picked up from Lester what he had learned in school, starting with the ABCs, and he taught me how to spell a few words. I was so happy when I could spell c-a-t, and after Mom taught me to count to one hundred, I felt ready to go to school. But I had to wait until the next fall.

It was about this time that Dad and Mom started calling Lester by his name rather than "Son," because I had been calling him that, too. I thought they had named him after the sun in the sky, and I visualized a shining, golden sun when I called him "S-u-n." There was so much for me to learn.

Mom taught us to be careful with matches by showing us what happened when she scratched the matchhead against a hard surface. A flame burst out, with which she lit paper in the cookstove to start a fire. We saw how quickly the flames flared up and burned the kindling. She told us to never strike a match unless we were starting a fire in the stove or lighting our kerosene lamps.

None of us ever set anything on fire in the house, except the time Dad accidentally knocked over a kerosene lamp. The glass globe broke, and the metal part holding the wick was loosened,

letting kerosene spill out on the wood floor. The lighted wick set
the kerosene on fire. Dad grabbed a small throw rug and tossed it
on the blaze, putting out the fire before it could do any damage. I
was glad only the globe of the lamp had shattered, and not the lamp
itself. It was my favorite — the one with the red peonies painted
on the side, that Dad had bought at an auction.

⇜ ⇝

Mom never forgot how much I liked that lamp and gave it to
me years later. I treasure it for the memories associated with it.
Besides, I still think it's pretty!

⇜ ⇝

Almost from the time we could walk, Lester and I had regular
chores to do. We had to keep the kitchen woodbox filled and
carried buckets of water to the house from the spring. When Mom
didn't have any chores for us to do, we climbed trees, rode horses,
jumped over the creek, picked wildflowers, played marbles, and
soared high into the sky on our swing.

The thick rope of the swing was fastened to a limb far up in
one of the trees in the front yard, and after we sailed sky-high into
the air, we discovered another game. Barefooted, we climbed the
ropes to the big limb above. Lester tried it first while I sat on the
seat of the swing to keep the ropes taut. He hooked his bare toes
around the ropes and "walked" up the ropes, pulling himself up
with his hands at the same time. When he came back down, it was
my turn. Soon I was sitting up on that limb about twenty feet off
the ground, surveying the world below.

When friends visited, Dad asked me to show them how I
climbed the ropes with my bare feet, while he sat on the swing to
keep the ropes tight. Eager to show off, I climbed up the rope to the

top limb as fast as I could. Our visitors seemed impressed! I decided to show them how fast I could come scurrying down. Instead of climbing down slowly, I loosened my grip with my hands and toes and slid lickety-split all the way down and straight into Dad's lap. It's a good thing he caught me, or I would have landed on the hard ground.

But no one had warned me about rope burns, and I learned all I wanted to know in that one quick slide. Although my fingers and toes were hurting, I was too sheepish to admit it in front of our visitors and didn't say anything about the burns until they left. Only then did I show Mom where the ropes had burned me. She gasped and ran to get the bag balm, a salve Dad used on the cows' teats when they became cracked. Mom daubed my fingers and toes with the soothing ointment, and the burns stopped hurting almost immediately.

The closest any of us ever came to hurting ourselves was the day Lester took a swig of *Black Leaf Forty*. Dad had warned us about it, saying it was a deadly poison, so Lester knew better than to drink it. Lester and I had gone with Dad to see Arthur Hyatt, and when we got to their house, we found several other kids playing with Buell and his brothers.

It wasn't long before the boys got to bragging about how tough they were. One of the older boys thought of a good way to prove it. He led us up the hill to the hay shed, and we went inside. Standing on his tiptoes, he reached up high for a bottle sitting on a two-by-four. Turning around, he showed it to us and said, "Lester, I'll drink some of this if you will."

The bottle had a picture of a skull and crossbones on it, plus some printing in big letters. Lester didn't want to admit he was afraid to drink it; they might call him a coward. So he tipped the bottle up and took a swallow. When he handed it back, the older boy backed out of the bargain.

It wasn't long before I noticed Lester lying curled up on the ground, looking sick. His black hair contrasted with sun-drenched green of the grass. Buell ran up to the house and told his mother what had happened. Mrs. Hyatt came hurrying down carrying a big bowl of beaten egg whites, knelt beside Lester, propped him up against her knee, and forced the egg whites down his throat. Her "medicine" worked. In just a few minutes, he threw up, getting rid of all the poison. Later, Dad told Lester, "I told you that was poison. It's a wonder you didn't die," sounding relieved as he said it.

The worst thing that befell us on the Hays Place happened in the first winter. When I got up one cold morning, I noticed Dad whispering to Mom when he came in from the barn. He went back outside again, carrying his rifle. I knew something was wrong when Mom kept Lester and me from following him. Soon we heard a loud bang, and Mom told us that Pansy, one of our milk cows, had gotten hurt trying to drink out of the creek, which was frozen solid. Pansy had slipped on the ice and broken a leg.

There was no way to set a cow's broken leg. Sad as it was, Dad had to get the animal out of her misery. I was not very happy — Pansy was pretty and gentle and had been my favorite cow. We were able to pet her without getting hurt, while the other cows tried to kick us or hook us with their horns. Since we couldn't afford to waste anything, Dad butchered the cow. I begged Mom not to tell me when she cooked the meat for dinner; I didn't want to know when I was eating Pansy.

Although Dad no longer had a job cutting down trees for a living, he did fell trees for firewood to keep the cookstove going and the house warm all winter long. The first tree he cut down was a tall old fir growing on the hillside below the house. Mom took Dora and me along to watch. Dad sawed and sawed all by himself with his two-man crosscut saw. After a while I looked up and saw the top of the tree beginning to sway back and forth. Scared that it would fall on us, I tried to jerk loose from Mom's hand and run home. But she held on to me as well as Dora and wouldn't let us move. She explained, "We're safe here. Dad knows just where the tree will fall because he has undercut it on one side. It will fall in that direction."

And sure enough, it did. The big tree crashed to the ground with a loud, earth-shaking thud right where Dad had said it would. I thought he was pretty smart to make a big tree fall where he wanted it to.

By this time, he had also learned a lot more about farming. That fall, when Howard Heidegger was threshing his grain, Dad, Ernest Keck and a couple of other neighbors joined to help him. Most of the farmers traded work among each other because no one could afford to pay extra help.

At noon, the threshing crew of five or six men came in for dinner and were having a lot of fun talking while they ate. Howard's wife, Opal, put steaming platters and bowls of food on the table and replenished them as the men helped themselves to seconds. She'd just refilled their cups with freshly brewed hot coffee, which Ernie Keck, involved in telling a long, drawn-out tale, hadn't noticed. He took a big gulp, burning his mouth. Turning away from the table, he spit the coffee the kitchen floor saying, "*There* now, damn you, blaze!"

Dad told us later that Ernie was embarrassed and ashamed and had apologized to Opal for spitting on her kitchen floor and swearing in front of her. He was a churchgoing man and didn't do much swearing, especially not in front of women.

5

River Crossing

"Tomorrow we're all going to the rodeo at Inchelium!" was Dad's surprise announcement one summer day. We had never been there, and the prospect of visiting a new place was exciting. We knew only that Inchelium was a small town across the Columbia River on the Colville Indian Reservation and could be reached either by driving upriver and crossing the bridge near Kettle Falls, or driving downriver past Rice and catching the ferry at Daisy.

❧ ❧

The ferry landing is now in a different place. It was moved after the Columbia River backed up from Coulee Dam.

❧ ❧

Going across on the bridge took more time but didn't cost anything. Since Dad drove our Star only twenty-five or thirty miles an hour on graveled roads, it would take nearly two hours — and would give us a dusty ride in our open car. Dad decided it was worth the one-dollar toll to cross the river on the ferry.

The thought of riding a cable ferry across the big river scared me. I remembered hearing that several years ago after a cable broke on a ferry above Kettle Falls, it had drifted helplessly downstream and gone over the falls. Everyone on board had drowned.

Just as we turned off the highway toward the landing, we saw the ferry heading our way, about fifty yards from the riverbank, where cars were already waiting in line to be carried across the big river. When the ferry docked, a worker tied ropes to posts at the river's edge, and laid down two heavy wooden planks to serve as the ramp for the cars to drive onto the ferry.

The planks bounced and shifted, making heavy thumping noises, when cars drove onto the ferry, and the attendant had to reposition the planks for each car. When all the automobiles were on board, he fastened a heavy chain across the back end of his load, and we slowly started to cross the river, while the workers collected the toll from each driver. A few people got out of their cars as we crossed, but we didn't budge. I felt a lot safer in the car.

When I realized the ferry was pulling itself across the half-mile stretch of turbulent river on just a cable, I really got scared. The cable bent in a big arc under the weight of the ferry and the current swung us downriver. I was afraid the cable would break before we reached the bank and we'd go floating down the river and over rocky rapids or dangerous falls, just as that other ferry had done.

But my fears didn't keep me from seeing the beauty of the land around me. Tall pine and fir trees covered the hills on both sides of the deep blue river. The rippling water sparkled in the sunshine, while wisps of clouds trailed gracefully across the summer sky, and snow-capped mountains touched the sky in the north.

Just the same, I was glad when we drew close to the shore and the ferry nosed up to the landing. The worker repeated his performance of tying the ferry to the landing, unhooking the chain in front of the cars and positioning the planks. When it was our turn, we drove off the ferry onto solid ground once again — and was I ever glad.

The Star chugged uphill on the dusty road the short distance to the rodeo grounds, and Dad found a spot to park. A lot of people were already sitting in the wooden bleachers on one side of the arena, watching the action. We found a bench with enough empty space for the five of us and sat down to watch the events.

Cowboys rode bucking broncos, trying to stay on the horse's back until the timer blew his whistle — only a few made it. Puffs of dust spurted up every time the horses' hooves pounded into the loose dirt, and when the cowboys lost their balance and sailed off their bucking mounts, more dust clouds whirled up when the unlucky rider hit the ground.

Calf roping was the next event. The contestant rode his horse into the corral, and as soon as the calf broke through the gate, the rider twirled his lasso and threw it around the calf's head, somersaulting the animal to a stop in a thick cloud of dust. The horse backed up, taking the slack out of the rope, while the rider jumped to the ground, the pigging string clenched in his teeth, and attempted to tie the calf's front leg to a back leg in record time. Whipping the string around, his hand made a blurred circle, working as fast as lightning. While waiting their turn, contestants practiced their roping skills by throwing the lasso at fenceposts and other targets, twirling loops over their heads before letting go.

Mom found a shady spot behind the bleachers, where we ate the sandwiches she had prepared, along with cold pop Dad bought from the concession stand. As the day wore on, the sun became hotter and the dust got thicker as it swirled and settled around us. We were sweaty, dirty and tired long before the rodeo was over. Mom breathed a sigh of relief when Dad finally announced, "Let's go home."

We had been happy to visit a new place. The rodeo had been exciting, but we had seen enough. Thinking about the return ride on the ferry didn't fill me with as much dread as it had earlier that morning. I just wanted to get home as fast as we could — even if it meant crossing that deep river on a small ferry.

⟨⟩ ⟨⟩

The last time Mom and I rode the ferry was in 1983, when the *Columbia Princess* (a modern ferry with a powerful engine) took us across the river on our way to visit Pat and Ernie McKinney in Keller.

6

Starting School

The day finally came when I started school. When Mom read stories to us, it always seemed like magic that she could tell what the funny markings on the pages meant. To me, they just looked like chicken scratches. Now I would soon know how to read, too!

Unlike the days I had watched Lester go to school, it was now my turn to go all the way up the road to the Pleasant Valley School. When Lester's friends stopped at our place on their way to school, I went along. I felt important, carrying my lunch pail just like the big kids. I knew how good the sandwiches in my quart-sized Karo syrup pail would taste at lunchtime, although I wasn't a bit hungry on my way to school. Instead of cooking oatmeal for breakfast, Mom had made wheat flakes and I had eaten two big helpings. After breakfast she prepared peanut butter sandwiches for our lunches, and for a treat she opened a can of deviled ham and made us each a sandwich. It tasted different than sandwiches made from leftover meat that we often had.

As we neared the grange hall, Hazel Rose joined our little group. It was her first day of school, too, and she was as excited as I was. A half-mile later a thrill went through me when we came into sight of the white frame schoolhouse. Hazel and I stood outside watching the classroom door for a glimpse of our teacher. Finally, at nine o'clock, Miss Dean opened the door and pulled the rope that rang the bell in the little white house atop the roof.

Miss Arlean T. Dean was our teacher for three years. In the past, when there were enough pupils to fill both rooms of the schoolhouse, there had been two teachers. But with only about twenty-five pupils, all eight grades shared the same room.

I loved Miss Dean from the first day. With her slim figure, dark wavy hair, and gentle voice, she was a beautiful lady to me. She taught us not to speak unless she asked us something — or we had a question about our work, to never interrupt and wait until she was between recitations. Although her voice was soft, she did not allow disturbances in her classroom. Lester and I knew better than to cause any trouble. Dad had told us if we got a spanking in school, he'd give us a harder one when we got home. Dad demanded instant obedience from us. When he swatted us for misbehaving, he felt he was only tapping us, but in reality, his "taps" were blows, which reminded us to behave ourselves and mind what he said. He never hugged us, but we knew he loved us, even though he never said so.

We went up to the recitation bench facing the teacher's desk for every subject. While one class was up front reciting, others studied at their desks getting ready for their turn. The higher grades went to the blackboards to write spelling words, work arithmetic problems and other lessons.

Miss Dean lived with her mother on the Root Place, about a mile from school, and arrived every morning in her little black coupe. She swept the oiled wooden floor of the schoolhouse, emptied the wastebasket into the stove, and assigned someone to fill the water bucket from the creek. On cold mornings, she started the fire in the iron stove.

⋖⋗ ⋖⋗

The Root Place was the farm we moved to in 1936. Since Dad and Mom later bought it, I've called it "The Home Place."

⋖⋗ ⋖⋗

The front door of the school led into a hallway, dividing the two classrooms. At the front door sat a square table with a water bucket on it. We all drank out of the tin cup hanging on a nearby nail. At the far end of the hallway a back door led outside — the shortest route to the girls' toilet. The boys used the front door, since their toilet was across the schoolyard.

In winter, we draped our mittens over the bumpers of the stove and set our overshoes — propped open — on the floor next to it. As mittens and overshoes dried, the odor of wet wool and warm rubber covered the usual classroom smell of oiled floor and chalk and spread through the whole room.

We wanted our things to be dry by recess when we went out to play our games and swing on the Giant Stride, which was our only playground equipment. Its sturdy metal pole stood about ten feet high, and the bottom was buried several feet deep into the ground, keeping it steady. The revolving top had chains suspended from it with a handhold at the end of each chain.

Five or six of us could swing at the same time, and I loved it! A running start made us fly around the pole, and brought our feet two or three feet off the ground. One day I saw Don Borland jump off while the rest of us were still whirling around, and I thought I could do it, too. But my timing wasn't as good as his. As I dashed out of the circle, a flying body rolled me to the ground, I saw stars and felt wobbly for a few minutes. I learned not to get off before everyone stopped.

In addition to swinging on the Giant Stride, we played all kinds of games, like pom-pom pullaway, three-cornered catch, antey-I-over, hide and seek and baseball. But the most fun I had in the first grade was at the Easter egg hunt. The Friday before Easter, Miss Dean brought a washtub full of beautifully colored eggs; and while we were studying, one of her friends hid them all over the schoolyard.

At recess, Miss Dean gave the first three grades a head start in the Easter egg hunt. We raced down the steps, eagerly searching for eggs in likely hiding places. Most of the kids made a dash for the far side of the playground, but I paused to look around and found my first egg, a blue one, behind the front steps. I hurried on and found more colored eggs behind rocks, in clumps of grass and behind bushes. It was exciting. Best of all, we got to take our beautiful eggs home with us.

At the end of the school year, in May 1931, I received a Certificate of Award for being neither tardy nor absent all year. It was signed, "Arlean T. Dean." I was as proud of my certificate as I was of having learned to read.

Miss Dean taught for two more years, and when she got married in May 1933, the school board didn't renew her contract. There was a rule against hiring a young married woman for a good reason. If the teacher became pregnant in mid-year, the board might have difficulty in finding a replacement. I was sorry she wouldn't be with us anymore. She had shown me that reading those "chicken tracks" was just as exciting as I'd imagined it would be.

7

Thunder in the River

Dad had announced he was hungry for smoked salmon. One of his Indian friends who was fishing in the cascades of Kettle Falls was just as hungry for meat from our freshly killed pig. The two men were going to make a swap. One afternoon, we made the twenty-mile drive to the falls in the Columbia River. Dad had told us that would see Indians catching salmon.

We crossed the rusty-looking iron-trussed bridge over the Colville River and saw the spot where it merged with the mighty Columbia. About three miles past the town of Kettle Falls, an automobile bridge and a railroad bridge spanned the Columbia River. Just short of the automobile bridge, Dad pulled off onto the shoulder, tires crunching gravel, and parked the Star at the side of the highway. We set off walking uphill.

Mom, heavy with child, held Dad's arm for balance as he led the way up the sandy hill, following wagon ruts that led to the Indian encampment. The powdery road dust felt warm on our bare feet as Lester, Dora and I trudged along behind, our feet sinking into the churned-up sand of the wheel tracks.

Topping the hill, we caught sight of about a dozen tepees, outlined white against the dark green of scattered pines. The teepees sat together on a knoll above the river, not far from St. Paul's Mission. I was only seven years old and thought all new things were exciting. Usually, Dad went alone on his trading trips. Letting all of us come along made it a rare adventure.

As we neared the encampment, we smelled the smoke from the campfires and heard bursts of happy laughter. The place was a confusion of sight and sound. Children whooped and hollered, dogs barked as they chased each other, racing in and out between the tepees, making the day seem like a holiday. Men with long braided hair, dressed in plaid shirts and overalls, walked up from the river carrying their catches of big salmon. Near the tepees, several women talked together while tending their cooking fires and watching over salmon drying on poles above the fires.

Each summer the Indians set up camp in northeastern Washington on the banks of the Columbia River alongside the falls. They came to catch the salmon going upstream to spawn and would stay until they had caught enough fish to last them through the winter. Some of the Indians lived nearby on the Colville Indian Reservation, while others came from as far away as northern Idaho and Montana.

Over the clamor of the camp's activities, I could hear the booming noise of the falls, and I slipped away from my mother's watchful eye to get a good look at the Columbia. I reached a rocky edge and stood looking down at the rushing water of the mighty river. The roar filled my ears, shutting out all other sounds.

Fascinated but frightened at the same time, my eyes stayed riveted on the racing current and the dangerous, swirling whirlpools thirty feet below me.

Upstream, several Indians were fishing along the riverbank. A few speared salmon from rickety wooden platforms jutting out into the rushing waters of the river. On the bank, others tended large handmade basket-like nets suspended near the cascades. Some of the leaping salmon landed in the baskets in their upstream run. A footbridge precariously connected the riverbank to a small, rocky island, where a half-dozen men perched on its jagged rocks, fishing for salmon.

The cascades' pounding and splashing filled my ears and kept me from hearing Mom's approach. All of a sudden, strong arms wrapped around my waist and jerked me backward, away from my perilous perch.

Later on Dad took me back to the river. He held my hand in a tight grip while I looked at the falls and the men fishing for their winter's food. There was so much to see. I'd never before beheld such a wondrous sight as these daring men netting and spearing the leaping salmon.

With the water level low in summer, I could see the large round holes — like kettles — in the rock ledges on the river bank, from which Kettle Falls got its name. Each spring brought high water during the runoff from melting snows in the Canadian Rockies. Over the years, the strong current had banged logs and trees onto the rocks, gouging out the deep "kettles."

At suppertime, Dad's friend gave us some salmon his wife had cooked over the fire. I held the warm chunk in my hand and ate slowly, feeling for bones with my tongue, careful not to swallow them.The juicy salmon tasted smokey like some of the fire was still there.

Darkness fell, and a different sound filled our ears. Finished with the day's work, the Indians had gathered to play the Stick

Game. With a small log in front of them, about twenty men and women sat on the ground in two lines facing each other across an open space. They used two sticks to hit the logs, making a clackety-clack-clack sound. A player on one team hid a small bone in one hand, and the other team tried to guess who had it.

I wondered what the clackety-clack of sticks had to do with this game that reminded me of Button, Button, Who's Got the Button? The clacking went on and on. Tired out from the long, eventful day, I lay in Dad's strong arms, contentedly watching sparks from the fires shoot up into the night sky. With the muffled roar of the falls in my ears, I was lulled to sleep by the rhythm of the sticks.

⋘ ⋙

It's been over sixty years since I saw the Indians gathered at the falls spearing salmon and playing their Stick Game. I can still see the tepee encampment and hear the clackety-clack-clack of the game, but can no longer smell the smoke.

8

Hays Hill Adventures

At Christmas that year we found two sleds leaning against the inside of the kitchen door. The varnish on their oak tops shone like a glare of ice in the sunlight. Unlike Dad's secondhand farm equipment, our sleds hadn't come from any auction sale — they were brand new. We hurried through breakfast, bundled up in our warm clothes, and ran outside to try out our presents. Zipping down the hill on our new sleds was just as exciting as we had imagined. The shiny runners took us downhill as fast as we wanted to go, and we didn't quit until we got tired of walking back uphill.

All through the winter we joined other kids in sleighing parties on the Hays Hill. Since there was hardly any traffic it didn't matter when we blocked the road off for a couple of hours. If a car came along, the driver waited until word was passed along the hill for everyone to stop coasting until he went by.

The kids living close to the Hays Hill loved it in the winter. The hill was steep enough to zip down at a fast clip, and it took only ten minutes to pull our sleds back up again. When the snow became hard-packed, we went so fast we couldn't stop until we got to the bottom. The high bank on our left was just a blur as we flew past.

Cars without chains that tried to make it up the hill would get stuck in the snow and had to be towed out. The hill was at its worst when the snow melted a little during the day, then froze again when the sun went down. The people living along the county road had to keep it plowed. Dad's section of a mile or two extended above and below our house and included the Hays Hill, which he kept plowed by pulling a homemade "Vee" behind his team of horses. A thin metal sheathing covered the front corner of the Vee, which reinforced it and kept the snow from sticking. Made of three planks, the contraption was almost as wide as our narrow county road and cleared the snow off in two runs. Dad walked behind it, guiding the team with the long leather driving reins.

Despite his efforts in keeping the road cleared, a few cars got stuck on the icy hill every winter, and he helped push them out of the snowy ruts. There were times when he had to hitch the team to the car and pull it up the hill.

He liked the Hays Hill better in the summertime because the steep pitch of the grade saved him from having to crank the Star to get it started. He kept the old car parked at the top of the rise, and when he wanted to go somewhere, all he had to do was turn on the switch, take it out of gear, let the brake off and push in the clutch. The car would slowly start rolling downhill, picking up speed as it neared the steep part of the grade, and the engine started all by itself.

Spring came, and we learned the Hays Hill could provide quite a bit of excitement without being covered by snow. Sam and Effie Curry came to visit, parked their open car off the road beside our little gate, and went into the house for a visit. Their two little girls, Arlene and Nadine, remained outside to play with Lester and me.

Sam hadn't had his car very long and was proud of its gleaming, shiny black finish. Newer than ours, his pride and joy didn't sit quite as high off the ground. With the snap-on curtains removed and the canvas top rolled back, the automobile looked like a roadster. Since it was newer and shinier than our car and seemed to be quite different in other ways, we started looking it over. Before long, Lester was standing on the running board, peering inside. He was curious about the big steering wheel, the pedals, gearshift and the other mysterious levers. Wanting to get a still closer look, he opened the front door and climbed onto the driver's seat. Naturally, I climbed in behind him, since I went almost everywhere Lester did. Dad had told us to never play in cars, but since we weren't going to play, only look, we thought it would be all right. Arlene and Nadine followed us and settled in the back seat.

Now that we were inside the car, we could examine it at close range. We were within reach of all the interesting-looking dials on the dashboard and the two long levers coming up from the floorboards. We sat quietly admiring everything for a few minutes, then Lester focused his attention on one of the levers. Wondering what it was for, he pushed it forward. When the car started moving slowly downhill, we found out what it was for — he had released the emergency brake!

Fortunately, Sam had seen the car moving and came racing out of the house. He cleared the fence in one stride and ran to overtake us. Jumping onto the running board, he reached in and yanked on the brake. The car jerked to a stop, and we were rescued from our runaway ride that could have ended in disaster.

Sitting in the front seat watching the steep grade getting closer and closer, I'd felt my face going white and had visions of us in a heap smashed up at the foot of the hill. We were all thankful Sam had caught up to us and pulled the emergency brake. If there had ever been a time to use it, this was it. It certainly was an emergency! Before Sam had jumped on the running board, the car had picked up speed and was nearing the steepest part of the hill. If we'd gone another twenty feet, we'd have been going so fast Sam wouldn't have been able to catch us.

Lester and I fully expected to get spanked for getting into the car and starting its downhill dash, but we escaped that, too. We guessed the only reason Dad didn't spank us was because he was as relieved as we were that the shiny car escaped damage and that we hadn't been killed.

Our investigation of Sam's car satisfied our curiosity. We never again climbed into a car again to "learn something new." In addition to learning about the brake, we realized Dad always had a good reason when he told us not to do something. We had felt helpless not knowing how to make the car stop.

We moved to a different farm a year later and Mom missed seeing all her friends who lived on the Pleasant Valley Road. Lester and I were able to keep in touch with our pals because we saw them every day in school. What we missed most was the winter excitement of sleigh riding down the Hays Hill.

⇦ ⇨

Many years ago the house on the Hays Place was torn down, leaving little to indicate where it once stood. The Hays Hill has been changed, too. The steepest part at the top has been graded down and fill added at the bottom. It's been tamed and no longer provides fun and excitement.

⇦ ⇨

While we lived on the Hays Place, our new baby sister, Leola Evelyn Riley, arrived on August 17, 1931.

When Mom's pains started, Dad drove her to Mrs. Julia Aldredge's Maternity Home in Kettle Falls, where most of the area women went to have their babies because it was closer and didn't cost as much as the hospital in Colville. Mrs. Aldredge called Mom's doctor, and shortly after Dr. Gray got to the maternity home, Leola was born.

Dad came home and told us Mom had a baby girl and had named her Leola Evelyn. Those were the fanciest names I'd ever heard. Mom told us later she had named our new sister after the characters in a novel she had read.

During Mom's absence, the house seemed empty, and when Dad finally brought her and the baby home ten days later, we were glad to see her. The house came to life again, and we all felt happy and content.

The tiny baby in Mom's arms looked like the doll Santa had brought me, except Leola was warm and soft, and I couldn't wait to hold her. I held out my arms, and Mom put my new sister on my lap. I felt the softness of her doll-like body as Leola squinted her eyes shut, opened and closed her mouth, and waved her tiny fists around while kicking her legs. When she opened her blue eyes and looked up at me, I knew she was going to be a lot more fun than my fancy doll that couldn't do anything but sit and look pretty.

Part III
1931 - 1936

The Curry Place

9

Move to the Curry Place

In late August 1931, we took over the Curry Place, which was located up the Heidegger Road beyond the Aldredge place, where we had stayed with Grandma — about seven miles from the Hays Place. Sam and Effie Curry moved away and offered to rent their farm to us. With about eighty of its 240 acres in cultivation, it was the biggest farm we had lived on. Lester and I weren't sure we were going to like the new place because it was about three miles as the crow flies from the schoolhouse. We had to walk — we sure couldn't fly!

Mom was sad to see Effie Curry leave. Only a few months before, her good friend Opal Heidegger had died. Mom was heartbroken — it was the first time I'd seen her cry. "I'm never going to have best friends again," she mourned, "as soon as I have one, she either dies or moves away."

Our new home sat at the end of the road and was isolated, with the Heideggers as our only neighbors. It was different from living alongside the Pleasant Valley Road, where cars went by every day and several neighbors lived close by. It also proved to be a long, long walk to school. The house, once a mustard-yellow color, was faded and streaked, with a small porch running across the front. Living room, kitchen and one bedroom were on the main floor, and a two-directional stairway led to two bedrooms upstairs, where Lester, Dora and I slept. Dad, Mom and the new baby used the downstairs bedroom.

The kitchen was just big enough to hold table and chairs and our big black cookstove. Since there was no sink, we had to carry water from the well. Unlike Abe and Margaret Heidegger, who had a generator to supply electricity, we had to be satisfied with kerosene lamps. There just wasn't enough money to buy a generator.

Lester and I took to the outdoors as we always did. The low branches of the big tree in the front yard made it a good climbing tree for us. When spring came, tall, candle-like blooms appeared and told us it was a horse-chestnut tree. After the blooms faded, big green-hulled balls formed with spikes all over them. When they ripened and dropped to the ground, we were elated to find shiny brown nuts under the prickly shells. Mom told us they were poisonous, but we could play with them. We were disappointed that we couldn't eat them, but we liked the chestnuts' rounded smoothness so much that we always carried a few in our overall pockets anyway.

There were two flowering bushes in the front yard. When the lilac was in bloom, we stuck our noses into the purple blossoms and breathed deeply, almost tasting their delicious fragrance. When the big white blossoms of the snowballs hung heavy on the branches, it was almost like looking at real snowballs that didn't melt in the sun.

A woodshed sat about fifteen feet from the side door, and beyond that was the cellar where we stored our canned fruits and vegetables, potatoes, carrots and squash. It was half-buried in the ground and stayed cool all summer long. Not far from that was the outdoor toilet. The blacksmith shop and barn were out from the front of the house, and a lean-to tacked onto one side of the blacksmith shop provided shelter for the Star. The barn was a hundred yards or so away and the barnyard smells didn't reach the house.

Like all the other places we lived before, we settled in quickly, were content and called it home.

11

By Horseback and Shanks' Ponies

I was standing in the middle of the corral where twenty feet away a big Hereford bull snorted and pawed the ground, sending up clouds of dust. Suddenly the big beast charged! He chased me around and around the corral. Every time I got close to the sides of the fence to climb over or duck through the horizontal poles, I heard his thundering hooves bearing down on me and felt his hot breath on my bare heels. My heart was racing, and my dry throat was gasping for air, but I didn't dare stop running. Then the bull lunged forward, butting me — and I jerked upright in bed. My heart was still pounding so hard I could hear it. But I was safe at home, thankful I had only been dreaming.

Although the big Hereford bull chased me only in my dreams, he was an ever-present threat to us as we walked to school. Our path led us right through the middle of Frank Rupert's cattle pasture, where his bull roamed loose. The few times Frank had him penned up in the corral by the barn, we knew we were safe and didn't have to keep on the lookout for him. But if we saw an empty corral and found the cattle grazing near our trail, we made a detour to steer clear of danger.

We thought all bulls were dangerous, so we kept our distance from this one. We had heard of a farmer near Rice who had been killed by his bull. Frank's bull never chased us, but we didn't trust him a bit and worried until we got safely through the small gate and into our own pasture.

Until Dora turned six, Lester and I made that long trek to school by ourselves. Little Dora was a spunky kid; she never whined or complained and kept up with us in spite of being so young. Our parents insisted we stay together and not ever get separated. We never considered that order a hardship; after all, we adventured together and had fun.

In the depth of winter, when Dad didn't need the workhorses on the farm, we rode them to school in less than one hour. But traveling by "shanks' ponies" — Mom's term for walking — took a lot longer.

We always took the shortest route to school because we didn't want to be late. Going home was a different matter, and when we felt adventurous we would take a detour or two. When we returned home on horseback we rode our horses to the barn and curried them to remove the dust and loose hairs. When we finally turned them loose in the corral, they shook themselves and ran around, kicking up their heels as though they'd just been let out of school, too. Lester's favorite horse was Pet, a frisky blue roan, while Dora and I rode double on Betty, a gentle sorrel mare. Dora wrapped her little arms around me and hung on for dear life all the way to school.

Hanging on was a good idea. We had to ride at a pretty good clip to keep up with Lester, who liked to gallop Pet and jump across ditches. We galloped and jumped, too, pressing our knees to Betty's sides. When she trotted hard, I had to grab a handful of mane to keep from falling off, while Dora hung onto me a little tighter.

Dora and I relied on Lester to keep us safe as well as be on the lookout for adventure. The day he was sick and hadn't gone to school, I had to be in charge. On our way home from school, it was cold and miserable, with a blizzard raging all around us. When we got to the big snowdrift on the trail, I found out just how much I had depended on Lester. He would have known what to do to make the horse go through the drift, but I had to manage on my own.

To make matters worse, we were riding young and frisky Pepper, a big black mare with long legs. She had been plodding through the knee-high snow at a steady pace. When we came out of the trees into the open field — where the icy wind bit into our faces and the swirling snow blew down our necks — Pepper stopped abruptly at the edge of a snowdrift, almost belly-high to her. The drift had completely covered the trail and continued across the field in a curving line, and snow kept blowing off the tops of drifts all across the open field. I kicked Pepper's sides with the heels of my heavy overshoes, but she refused to go through the drift.

I kicked again, and I slapped her with the reins. When she remained standing at the edge of the drift, I remembered Lester saying that if you give a horse its head, it will know which way to go. We slid off her back, I let go of the reins, and Pepper immediately skirted the highest part of the drift and high-tailed it toward the barn, a quarter-mile away. She plowed through the deep snow on her long legs with ease and a lot faster than I could go.

Stiff with cold and hampered by the snow, I hurried a few awkward steps before realizing I wouldn't be able to catch her. I was mortified that I hadn't thought to stay on Pepper and give the reins enough slack so she could pick her own trail. Dora and I were thoroughly chilled; our hands and faces were ice-cold and stinging.

Sitting on Pepper's back had at least kept our bottoms and legs warm. Snow was getting inside our overshoes, making our ankles numb. Our pantlegs got wet, then froze stiff, making a rasping sound with each step we took. The snow continued blowing in our faces as we followed Pepper's trail downhill.

❧ ❧

Talking about this recently with Kit (Dora), she confessed she had thought she really *was* going to freeze.

❧ ❧

Our parents had been watching for us from the kitchen window. Worried when they saw Pepper coming down the hill alone, Dad immediately set off on foot to find us. We were glad to see him coming up the trail, even though we had topped the hill and could see our house with smoke coming out of the chimney, making it look all snug and warm in the blowing wind.

Dora went straight into the house, and I started following Pepper to the barn to let her in and to feed her some hay. Dad astonished me by saying, "I'll put Pepper in the barn and take care of her. You go on into the house and get warmed up." Taking care of the horses after a ride was our responsibility. As I went into the house, I felt a bit guilty for shirking my duties.

When we took our mittens off in the house, our hands were blue. Mom was afraid we might have frostbite. She wouldn't let us go near the stove so we wouldn't warm up too fast. Our hands turned red, and started hurting. We had been cold lots of times, but our hands and faces had never tingled and stung like this before. We hoped we'd never get that cold again.

Carrying our lunches in paper bags was a nuisance, and Mom made us denim shoulder bags from the legs of worn-out overalls.

We slung these handy lunch bags around our necks and forgot about them. They worked out a lot better than the flimsy paper bags and gave us freedom to hang onto the reins and the horse's mane.

It was my job to make lunches for the three of us. For one sandwich, I mixed Karo syrup and peanut butter together. For the other, I used leftover venison steaks, which tasted great between slices of homemade bread. When Dad heard me complaining to Mom one day about having the same old things every day, he said when he was a boy, his sandwich consisted of lard spread between two slices of bread.

That made me more appreciative of my sandwiches for a while, but toward the end of a week, I got tired of cold venison steak on dry bread. The tallow from the cold meat stuck to the roof of my mouth, and I could hardly swallow the dry bread. I traded half of it for a strawberry jam sandwich on store-bought bread. When I got hungry in the early afternoon, I regretted my trade. Jam sandwiches just didn't stick to my ribs like meat. I never made that mistake again, and somehow I never told Dad, who would have been glad to have had a venison sandwich instead of lard spread between slices of bread.

One bitter-cold winter morning, Dad came in from milking and offered to take us to school. "It's too cold for you to go by yourselves, either walking or riding," he said. Without a thermometer, telephone or radio, we had no way of knowing just how cold it was. But Dad could tell it was much colder than usual. On his walk back from the barn, the severe cold had pinched his nose almost shut, and the snow crunched squeaky under his rubber boots. He and Lester harnessed two horses and hitched them to the big bobsled — our low wagonbed mounted on a double set of runners, filled with straw for warmth. Mom heated some flatirons on the kitchen stove, wrapped them in old pieces of overalls, and spread a quilt around us, and we snuggled down behind Dad in the wagon seat.

We had barely gone a quarter of a mile uphill when white frost settled all over the horses' noses and chests. Dad stopped the team, got off, and held his hands over their nostrils to thaw the ice off their muzzles. When he got back on the sled, his black three-day-old stubble of beard had turned white, too.

When we arrived at school, there was no one there. The Heideggers' house sat across the creek from the schoolhouse, and Raymond had seen us pull up. After greeting us, Raymond asked Dad, "Bill, didn't you know it was thirty-six degrees below zero this morning? School has been cancelled until this cold weather breaks." We turned around and headed back home, glad we hadn't ridden the horses that day. It would have been a miserable ride for nothing.

Winters were hard in our part of the country, and we wore long-sleeved and long-legged wool underwear, warm flannel shirts and bib overalls. Dora and I had a struggle every morning making the legs of our underwear stay down while pulling on our cotton stockings. We hated the lumps the thick folds of the underwear made under our stockings, but we had to put up with it.

We also hated wearing the itchy old underwear after the temperature got above freezing. In late winter, after we enjoyed a couple of warmer days, we always tried to convince Mom we no longer needed the bulky underwear, since we now had warm weather. But she prevailed and told us we had to keep them on until spring. Mom was always right. We had another cold spell and, walking home in the snow and wind, we were glad she hadn't been fooled by our "warm weather" story.

When spring came, beautiful blue rock flowers bloomed and big patches of sunflowers covered the slope we passed on our way to school. In late spring, yellow blossoms grew out of each clump of long, grayish-green arrow-shaped leaves less than a foot high. By fall the leaves became stiff and dry and faded to a whitish-gray, and when the wind tossed and bounced them in its wake, they rubbed together and sounded like the rattling of a snake.

❧   ❧

My daughter, Janet Eileen, tells me the real name of these sunflowers is "arrowroot balsam." Now when I spot them on my drive across Central Oregon's high desert to visit her, my eyes pick out their unique clumps, and I remember their rattling in the wind.

❧   ❧

One fall day as we walked through the sunflower patch on our way home from school, we heard a rattling sound and thought it was the wind blowing the leaves. As the rattling continued, Lester held up his hand for Dora and me to stop. We looked in the direction where the sound came from but saw nothing except dry sunflower leaves. Finally we spotted the rattlesnake lying coiled and holding his rattle slightly above his mottled body, his narrow head with its beady eyes pointed straight at us. His rattle was vibrating so fast we could just see a blur.

Quickly we grabbed some rocks, aimed at the head, hit our target and soon had killed it. With the toe of his shoe, Lester nudged the limp body. Convinced the snake was dead, he cut off its rattle with his jackknife.

We were so excited, we ran most of the half-mile distance to the house to show the rattle to Mom and Dad. We told them about spotting the rattler and killing it, feeling proud to have gotten rid of something so dangerous. Dad remarked that our rattlesnake wasn't as old or as big as some, but was just as poisonous. After we all took turns shaking the rattle to hear the rasping noise and had counted the segments again, Lester dropped it in the saucer with the several other rattles we had collected.

Walking home from school, we occasionally stopped to see how Art Bovee was progressing in his "mine." He had dug a hole in the hillside looking for ore. Sometimes he and his wife, Jessie, had enough money for dynamite, but most of the time they just used their picks, shovels and crowbars to make headway. It's not certain they ever discovered what they were after. All I could ever see was water dripping continuously out of the hole's ten-foot ceiling, making big puddles on the stony ground. It was a gloomy place, and I was always glad to leave.

We had heard coyotes howling, so Dad had set traps in the hope of catching them, as well as muskrat, coyote, or mink and selling their pelts. We were to check the traps and bring the catch home. One day, walking through the aspen grove, we heard a noise and saw a coyote caught in a trap, jumping up and down trying to get loose. We didn't dare take the coyote out of the trap while it was still alive. Lester managed to kill the coyote by hitting it on the head with a heavy stick. We took turns packing the heavy carcass home and knew we had saved Dad a long walk to check on his traps.

Not all of our trips back home from school by shanks' ponies were that exciting. Most of the time it was just a lot of hard walking, but we were always on the lookout for what we called adventures. When Frank Rupert told us that one of his cows had lost her bell, we decided to look for it. Lester was the one who found the cowbell. All three of us went straight to Frank's house to give it to him, and we told him where Lester had found the bell. Frank was so pleased to get it back that the next time he drove to Colville, he bought a sack of candy for us. We hadn't expected a reward, but store-bought candy didn't come our way very often and was a special treat. We thanked him and hurried home to share it with the others.

Not only did we like the Ruperts, but we loved their dog Sport, who became a special friend. He was one smart animal. At milking time Frank would call for the dog, wave his arm in the direction of the cows, and say, "Go get the cows, Sport."

Sport would streak out to the pasture, circle around behind the cows, and get them started for the barn. He never chased them, just walked behind them and kept them going. Sport always met up with us on our way home from school and ran alongside us with leaps and bounds, knowing we'd stop to pet him. After we moved away, Frank told Dad how much Sport missed us. "He still waits in the lane every day for those kids, acting puzzled because they don't come by. He even runs up and down the road looking for them."

One day Frank told Dad that the dog had died unexpectedly, without having been sick. "I think he just died of a broken heart." We were all sorry we hadn't taken Sport to live with us — we had missed him, too.

• • •

While living on the Hays Place, I had won a Certificate of Award for being neither tardy nor absent all year. But I was prouder of the one I received from Miss Dean in 1933 after we had moved to the Curry Place. The trail had been a long one, and it hadn't always been easy to get to school on time by horseback or shanks' ponies.

Our Neighbors, the Heideggers

The first time we visited the Heideggers' since we moved to the Curry Place, Abe Heidegger handed me a big white seashell and told me to hold it up to my ear and listen to the sounds of the ocean. I looked at the pinkish glow inside the shell and pressed it against my ear. Sure enough, I could hear the sound of a distant ocean. When it was Lester's turn, I watched his eyes widen at such magic. At seven and nine years of age, it was easy to believe (almost) we could hear the rushing waves of an ocean hundreds of miles away.

We were just as fascinated with the dried-up yellow starfish Abe brought out for us to see. We had never seen this creature before. Just to look at it and touch all its arms — feeling its stiff, bumpy body — was worth the long walk to the Heidegger house.

We were always happy when Mom sent us on an errand to the Heideggers. Sometimes we delivered a message, other times she borrowed something. She was too busy cooking, canning and taking care of baby Leola to go herself. Without a telephone, she relied on one of us to do the running for her. Since we didn't see many people in the summer, we were only too glad to go, and perhaps get another look at their treasures from the ocean.

The Heideggers' two-story, white house was larger than ours and had a wide front porch that wrapped around two sides, making the whole house look cool and inviting in the summer. Unlike our house, the Heidegger place had screens on all the windows and doors, which kept most of the flies out. Another attraction was the platform glider in the front yard. Painted white, it sat next to a bed of moss roses. Sitting on seats facing each other, Lester and I loved swinging on it to see how high the glider would go without tipping over. It never fell over, but it did come off its base a time or two, and we had to lift it back into place again. Abe and Margaret never scolded us or acted cross, even when we deserved it, or when I lied to him that day in his cherry orchard.

Mom had sent me to the Heideggers' orchard to pick a bucket of bing cherries. I had filled my bucket and was about to return home when a young shirttail relative of Abe's rode a horse into the orchard and invited me to go for a ride with her. I never turned down an offer to ride, and I swung up behind her. From a slow trot through the orchard the horse's gait changed, and all of a sudden we galloped through the rows of trees, kicking up clouds of dust and dirt that settled on the people picking cherries and into the baskets full of the rich, red fruit.

We heard angry yells, but no one made us stop. A man climbed down a ladder and went up to the house. I suspected he was going to tell Abe on us —with good reason. I knew we were doing something wrong, and I wasn't surprised to see Abe striding purposefully toward us, looking around, taking in the dust-covered trees. Upon reaching us, he asked, "Have you been galloping through the orchard?"

My friend spoke up quickly. "No, we haven't," she lied.

Not wanting to contradict her, even though she hadn't told the truth, I chimed in, saying, "Oh, no."

Instead of scolding us, Abe quietly told us to take the horse out of the orchard. He made it seem like it was the horse's fault for kicking up all that dust. He knew we hadn't told the truth, and I was lucky he didn't tell my parents. I'd never lied to them, even when I had done something I knew was wrong. That was one of the few times I deserved a spanking and didn't get one — maybe it made up for those I didn't have coming.

Three summers later, Lester and I got into a different kind of trouble when we decided to go help Abe's hired hand, Marvin Tracy, who was digging in the hillside in search of water, which Abe planned to pipe down to the barn. The prospective spring was dug into the slope of a series of hills which were covered with straw-colored cheat grass in the summer.

Bored after finishing our morning chores one day, Lester and I wandered over to see how Marvin was coming along with his digging. Climbing up the hill was hard work. Tilting above us, the hill seemed to get steeper the higher we got. My leg muscles ached with every step, and my throat was so dry I could hardly swallow.

When we finally got to the top, Marvin was outside the short tunnel, tossing big rocks into a heaping ore cart sitting on the tracks. He gave us a welcoming grin and said, "I'll bet you walked all the way up here just to help me, didn't you?"

He produced a big jug of water, took a drink, and offered it to us.

Marvin must have been lonely because he seemed glad to have company and liked joking around with us. We had liked him right off when we saw a happy smile crossing his face. He always had something funny to say and enjoyed talking to us as much as he did with grown-ups. That was the reason we had gone to help him.

I peered into Marvin's dusty-walled tunnel, which was about ten feet long and reminded me of a mine. I wondered how he was going to hit water in such a dry hillside. We asked what we could do to help, and he told us to push the ore cart piled high with rocks down the track.

With Lester on one side of the cart and me on the other, we put our shoulders against the back end and started heaving. The cart was so heavy we had to push with all our might to get it rolling, and kept pushing as hard as we could to keep it going. The ore cart suddenly ran off the end of the tracks and tipped over, spilling the rocks. Marvin would have to find a way to haul the heavy cart back up the hill and get it mounted on the tracks once more. At that point, figuring we had "helped" Marvin enough, we told him goodbye and took off for home. We never learned how our friend lifted the ore cart back up onto the tracks. Considering the fact he might be mad at us, we didn't want to remind him of all the extra work we had caused him.

❧ ❧

Fifty-five years later, Ruth Heidegger wrote about the well-digging efforts. "We didn't find enough water to make it worthwhile for all the work they did up there."

She added that her Grandfather Coppinger raised broom corn at their place. He made excellent brooms from it and sold them."

13

Baby Sister Effie

The maternity home was located in Mrs. Aldredge's small brown house in Kettle Falls, where she lived with her teenage daughter, Janiece. Not only was the maternity home more convenient to reach, but Mrs. Aldredge didn't charge as much as the hospital did. Dr. Gray, unable to drive all over the country to deliver babies, met the expectant mothers at the maternity home.

When Mom started labor pains, Dad headed to Kettle Falls, leaving us kids home alone. He stopped at the Heideggers' and told them where he was taking Mom, and Ruth Heidegger promised to stay with us until he returned. With Ruth around, we cleaned house first, and when Dad hadn't come home by suppertime, Ruth fixed a meal from our stock of canned foods. After supper we helped clean the kitchen and Lester filled the woodbox. When Leola started getting cranky, we realized we had forgotten to put her to bed.

Still, Dad had not returned. It seemed like he had been gone a long time. Finally, twin beams of car lights cut into the darkness of the woods below the house and proceeded up the road. At last Dad was home. Coming in the door, he said, "Well, we have us another girl," and left to drive Ruth to her house.

We were excited about our new baby sister and wanted to see her the next day. But we had to wait three days until Dad finished planting grain — that chore could not wait.

We arrived at Mrs. Aldredge's place and, feeling nervous in strange surroundings, we four kids tagged along behind Dad as he opened the gate that led to Mrs. Aldredge's Maternity Home. We hadn't been there for over two years — not since Leola arrived. Now we had another baby sister, born May fifth, 1933.

As we entered the large room, we saw Mom and two other women lying in narrow beds, but there was no sign of babies anywhere. We hugged our mother, and she asked us how we were getting along. Lester told her we were doing all our regular chores, plus helping Dad with the cooking. Dora and I had been taking care of Leola as well as washing dishes and sweeping the floors. Finally, Mom detected our curiosity, and she pointed to three bassinets lined up behind a partition in the next room and said, "Your little sister is the one on the left."

Looking at all the babies, we decided ours was the prettiest one. She was just as pretty as her name, Effie Eileen Riley. Mom had decided she would name a girl after Effie Curry, her best friend, and Eileen for the enchanting heroine in a story she had read.

Mom couldn't come home with us yet. Dr. Gray insisted she stay at Mrs. Aldredge's for ten full days. He knew she wouldn't be able to get much rest at home with five children to care for and no washing machine. We were glad when she and the baby came home. Once again, our house felt warm and complete.

For a few days, we eagerly took turns holding our new baby sister when she was awake. Looking into her smoke-colored eyes, we wondered whether they'd be brown like Mom's, or blue like Dad's and the rest of us. We also wondered what color her hair would be. Effie's hair was almost black, but so was Leola's before it turned blonde. Since our parents had dark hair, we asked Mom where the blonde hair came from. She said, "We must have a blonde ancestor somewhere."

Mom showed Dora and me how to hold Effie up to our shoulders and burp her after her bottle, and how to change diapers. When Effie was fussy, we held and cuddled her until she went to sleep. Young as we were, we pitched in and helped with the baby as well as with the housework.

When Effie was a year old, she disappeared one day when no one was watching her. Mom came running through the door, her words rushing together. "I can't find Effie anywhere in here — she must have slipped outside when I wasn't looking. Go see if you can find her."

Lester took off at a run for the granary, barn and blacksmith shop; Dora headed around the corner of the house to look in the woodshed, the cellar and the garden behind the house. Always fearful of the wells, I made a beeline for the one near the road, terrified that Effie might have fallen in. Although we never used water from that well, it was uncovered. I knew she wasn't big enough to climb over the framework around the well, but that still couldn't keep me from worrying.

Calling her name as I hurried along, I reached the well and looked down into the dark water, calling to her again. All I could see was the frightening, still dark water below. Suddenly I felt foolish for standing over the well calling her name. If Effie had fallen in, it wouldn't do any good to call. Since she wasn't around the first well, I ran the hundred yards to the other one. She wasn't there, either, so I ran back to the house to see if anyone had found her.

Just as I got there, Lester returned from his search, and Dora came around the corner of the house from the opposite direction. Neither had seen Effie. We ran into the house, and as soon as we got into the kitchen, someone spotted Effie's little blonde head poking out from under a pile of clothes — she was sound asleep on top of the stack of ironing. One of Dad's blue workshirts covered all but the top of her head. No wonder Mom hadn't been able to find her. We would have to keep our eyes on that baby!

❧ ❧

A letter from Goldie Entwistle in 1991 tells about three of her children being born at Mrs. Aldredge's Maternity Home.

"Gerry, Bill and Janice were born at Mrs. Aldredge's. Janiece Aldredge helped her mother and was a pretty good nurse for a young high school girl. When 'Jenny' was born with all that red hair, I named her after Janiece Aldredge, who had flaming red hair. But in spelling her name on the birth certificate, the first 'e' got left out, resulting in 'Janice,' instead of 'Janiece.'"

Several years after Janiece Aldredge had helped her mother in the maternity home, she married Goldie Entwistle's only brother, Ted Smith.

14

Exploring the Hills

Growing up on a farm, living on the land surrounded by open spaces, there was much to be explored. Having finished our morning chores, Lester, Dora and I followed our favorite pastime of roaming the hills. There were over one hundred acres too rocky, too steep, or too wooded to plow. Although no good for farmland, this wild area served as pastureland for the cows, sheep and horses. Like a magnet, the land drew us to it and became our playground and unlimited source of our adventures.

"Come see what I found," Lester called excitedly one day. "I told you we'd find that killdeer nest if we tried hard," he added as we looked down at the four small eggs nestled inside a circle of pebbles. On that patch of rocky ground the spotted eggs looked so much like pebbles that Dora and I had gone right past the nest without seeing it.

A few minutes earlier we had laughed as the mother killdeer tried to fool us into chasing her by acting like she had a broken wing. As soon as we saw her flopping around, half running and half flying, we knew her nest was close by. Killdeers made their nest on the ground among the rocks instead in the trees like all our other feathered friends.

In roaming the hills, we came across a robin's nest, among others. I climbed up the tree for a better look, and I heard a flutter of wings above my head. Mother robin had taken flight. I climbed higher until I could see into the nest, and discovered three blue eggs, and one of them had a crack in it. Not wanting to keep the mother robin away from her nest too long, I dropped from the branch and we left, continuing on up the hill to see what else we could find.

For the next three weeks we checked the robin's nest and saw the eggs hatch. At first the baby birds couldn't open their eyes, and they were scrawny, naked little things with big heads wobbling on their skinny necks. They didn't have feathers yet and only a few straggly hairs stuck out of their pale, wrinkled skin. But it wasn't long before feathers covered their nakedness. Soon all we could see were three gaping mouths flung open, ready for the bits of angle-worms we dropped in.

Another day in late spring, our roaming brought us a rare and unexpected treat: we came across a pond. We had crashed through a thicket of quaking aspen and came out in a small clearing. Water from melting snow had gathered, forming a temporary pond, which looked deep enough to go wading.

Throwing off our clothes down to our underpants, we ran into the sun-warmed water. Splashing around, we tried to swim, knowing we couldn't drown since the water was only waist deep. We played until it was time to go home. Reluctantly, we put our dry clothes on over our wet underpants and headed home. We never told Mom about our discovery, because we were afraid she wouldn't let us go back. All set to go "swimming" again the following week, we returned to the quaking aspen thicket. But there would be no swimming — our pond was gone. It had dried up.

We spent so much time roaming the hills that we knew where and when the wildflowers were blooming. The little white spring beauties were first, then came the shiny yellow buttercups, fuchsia shooting stars, yellowbells, bluebells, columbines, sunflowers, lavender-blue rock flowers and bushes of serviceberry and syringa blossoms. Indian paintbrush and mariposa lilies came last, blooming in the summer. The circles on the lavender-pink petals of the mariposa lilies made them look like butterflies tied to the ground on stems.

All the flowers were pretty, but we liked the tubular-shaped rock flowers best of all. We called them "blue rock flowers" because they grew only in the rockslide on the far side of the farm. From a distance, the masses of bloom made the broken pieces of jagged grey boulders appear lavender-blue.

Tied down in the house with babies, Mom couldn't go wandering around to see the flowers, so we brought them to her. The first time we took branches of the creamy-white, fragrant syringas to her, she breathed in their fragrance, thanked us, and exclaimed with delight, "Oh, that's the state flower of Idaho! Some call it 'mock orange' because it smells like orange blossoms."

When our wanderings led us near big pine trees, we looked for clumps of pine gum, which was a liquid that oozed out between the cracks in the bark and hardened into round reddish-brown lumps. The oldest and darkest pieces made the best-tasting gum, which had a woodsy flavor that store-bought gum didn't have. If we found more than we could chew at once, we stuck the pieces in our overalls pockets and saved them for another time.

One afternoon when we had run out of exciting things to see in the hills, Lester came up with something new. He started climbing a willowy aspen about twenty feet tall. He looked down at us and said, "I'm going to see if I can make this tree bend down to the ground."

He climbed as high as he could to the limber upper part, still hanging on, and jumped out away from the trunk of the tree. The tree bent over with his weight until his toes were only two or three feet off the ground. After the tree stopped swaying him back and forth, he swung his legs back to the tree trunk. The tree swayed down, and this time his feet almost touched the ground. He flew back and forth, each flight becoming shorter, until the tree ran out of motion. His arms were tired of hanging on, and he climbed down. "Boy, that was fun," he said. "Why don't you try it?"

Picking a tree that was skinnier and not as tall as the one Lester had ridden, I climbed to the top. When it started bending, I hung on tight with my hands but let go with my legs and sort of lurched out from the tree. Swaying back and forth *was* fun! The next time, I rode my slender tree down until my feet touched the ground, then hung on as it whipped back and forth. Lester said, "If you can touch the ground, I can, too."

But his wild ride ended up with the tree flipping him off, and he fell to the ground, landing hard. Dora and I went over and knelt beside him. A little blood trickling out of his ear made me wonder if he had killed himself. But after a couple of minutes, he staggered to his feet, looking dazed. We decided to give up our tree riding for that day.

One long summer day when we didn't feel ambitious enough to go exploring, we went past the barn to look at the Columbia River, far below. Lying sprawled out on the ground, we followed the wet blue-ink ribbon of river as it headed south in a soft zig-zag pattern. The tree-covered mountains on the other side in Ferry

County were to the west. To the north were more mountains, which Dad said were in Canada. It was quite the view.

All of a sudden Lester caught a grasshopper and held it with its head facing him. He had heard they could do a special trick. He squeezed its jaws, saying, "Spit tobacco juice, spit tobacco juice."

Sure enough, some dark brown juice oozed out of the grasshopper's mouth. I caught one and, squeezing its head, I said, "Spit tobacco juice." And it did — after I squeezed a little harder. They probably would have oozed brown juice even if we hadn't said the magic words.

Another bug that got our attention sometimes was the doodlebug. These were tiny, dusty-gray bugs that lived at the bottom of cone-shaped holes in soft dirt. The pincers on their heads helped them catch tiny insects and bugs that fell into their holes. It was fun to see if we could fool a doodlebug into thinking something had fallen into the hole and was trying to climb out the smooth sides.

"Doodle, doodle, doodle, doodle," we droned, leaning over with our mouths close to the hole. After about a minute of droning, I could see a slight movement in the loose dirt at the bottom of the hole. Repeating my "doodle, doodle" until the doodlebug stuck its head up out of the dirt, I quickly scooped it up with a splinter of wood. After coaxing it out to prove I could trick it, I dropped it back into its hole.

It was during these times of boredom that we did things we weren't supposed to do, like smoking. Our parents didn't smoke. But when we found a flat pack of cigarette papers that one of Dad's friends had left behind, we decided we had to see what smoking was like. Lester had it all planned. "We'll go get some Indian tobacco that's growing out by the pigpen. It's all dry and brown and looks just like tobacco, even if the seeds are larger."

It didn't take us long to strip a handful of dry, brown seeds off the dock plant — our Indian tobacco. Lester demonstrated how he'd seen a man roll his cigarette. Pouring some of the brown dock seeds onto the thin white tissue, he said, "All you have to do is spread it out along the paper, then roll the paper around the tobacco and lick it to seal it."

After licking the long edge of the paper, he held his cigarette up for me to admire. It was an uneven, lumpy object that only faintly resembled a cigarette. He handed one of the thin papers to me for rolling my own.

I followed suit and came up with something that looked even less like a cigarette than his did. He dug a match out of his pocket and lit the end of our "cigarettes." We sucked on them, just like we'd seen the men do. It took all of three big puffs to convince me that this wasn't as much fun as it looked. My tongue was on fire — just like the blazing tip of my cigarette.

Neither of us liked the results of our first try at smoking, but that didn't keep us from trying it again. We made more cigarettes than we smoked and became so good at rolling our own that they almost looked like real cigarettes. A few even stayed glued together after we licked them.

The only time we tried to smoke real tobacco taught me a good lesson. We had found an old cigar that a friend, after the birth of a baby, had given to Dad. After taking a few puffs, I stopped, and handed the cigar to Lester. It tasted worse than our homemade cigarettes, and all of a sudden I didn't feel very good. Looking at me, Lester told me that my face was turning green. That didn't surprise me. I *felt* green, and a minute later I threw up. When I felt better, I swore I'd never smoke another cigar. Getting sick that day cured me of smoking for life, and we almost lost interest in gathering "tobacco" and rolling our own.

But we never lost interest in our homemade slingshots, which we carried with us everywhere, even to school. The first one Lester had was made from a "Y" branch he brought home from a hunting trip with Dad. I nagged him to make a slingshot for me.

We set out to look for a forked branch just the right size. "You don't want one too small or it'll break, or one so big you can't grip it," Lester advised. We kept on looking until we ended up with three forked branches.

We cut the prongs the length we wanted and peeled the bark off. From a worn-out inner tube, we cut two rubber strips to attach to the prongs. We used a small piece of leather from the tongue of an old boot for the part that held the rock. When we had it fastened to the free end of the rubber strips, our slingshots were ready to use.

We knew better than to shoot at the chickens or any of our farm animals, but there were plenty of good targets. We aimed at snakes, ground squirrels, yellow-jacket nests, fenceposts, knotholes, puddles of water, or just target circles we drew in the dirt. Using our slingshots was easier on our arms than throwing rocks, and we could shoot straighter, too. We kept our slingshots in our hip pockets at our fingertips — ready to use when a likely target crossed our path.

Our summertime roaming was plagued by encounters with tar weeds and cheat grass, which got down into our shoes and caught in our socks and pantlegs. The small round stickers on the tar weeds were sharp and stickery and had to be picked off one by one. Cheat grass heads weren't quite so bad, but they took longer to pick out as they worked their way into our knit socks with their prickly points digging into our skin. I wished for high-topped shoes like Lester's, which gave more protection from cheat grass and tar weeds and also kept small rocks from getting down the backs of my shoes when I slid down the hills.

In winter we couldn't roam around the hills for fun like we did in summer. About all we could do was ride our sleds, make snowmen, or show Leola how to make snow angels. She laughed, thinking it funny to see us lying on our backs in the snow making "wings" with our flailing arms. When bad weather kept us cooped up, we'd play checkers or dominos, but that wasn't nearly as much fun as roaming the outdoors.

It was exhilarating to see spring approach and watch the snow disappear. We could go exploring the hills and see new life start all over again.

❧ ☙

I still like my special pine gum and look for it every time I'm in a forest of big pine trees. There's a row of doodlebug holes in the dirt under my back porch. Lately I've had a strange urge to stoop down, say, "doodle, doodle," and see if I can still trick one into showing himself.

Pleasant Valley Grade School

Mrs. Ethel Graham became our teacher for all eight grades the fall Lester and I were in fourth grade and Dora started first grade. We were curious what she would be like. We knew she was old — older than any of our parents — and that she and her husband Billy had recently moved into a cabin up above John Byrd's farm. Henry Higgins joked that because of her age and her name, he would greet her with, "Good morning, Teacher, how is your old *gray ham*?"

When the school bell rang that morning, we hurried inside, eager to satisfy our curiosity about the new teacher. As soon as I saw the dark piercing eyes in a stern-looking face, I didn't think Henry would have the nerve to ask Mrs. Graham about her "gray ham" or make any other smartalecky remark. Her manner indicated without any doubt she was used to keeping order in her classroom and wouldn't stand for any nonsense.

"Good morning, children, take your seats," were her first words.

Mrs. Graham was a slim older woman who stood stiff as a poker in her dark skirt and white blouse. Tight marcelled waves of gray hair went all around her head. Behind steel-rimmed spectacles, her sharp eyes sorted us out. Standing beside her desk at the front of the room, she gave us her instructions. "The first graders will sit in the row next to the stove, and the eighth graders in the row next to the window. Pupils in the other grades will sit at the desks in between for now. Next week, I'll assign specific desks."

She sat down at her own desk, her back stiff and straight, and called roll. As we answered, "Here," when our names were called, her eyes tracked down the voice and studied our faces, as if determined to put a face with the name.

After seeing Mrs. Graham standing tall and straight all the time, it came as no surprise that she expected us to have good posture. Whenever I slumped over a book, she'd appear, telling me to "Sit up straight, Ines. Don't slouch in your seat."

Since she was the only teacher for the thirty or more pupils in all eight grades, she kept an eye on all phases of our education. She pointed out every misspelled word on our papers, whether they were geography, history or spelling. It didn't make any difference which subject it was; all the words had to be spelled correctly. The same was true of punctuation and grammar.

That November we got to do something we had never done before. Mrs. Graham announced we were going to put on a Christmas program at the grange hall. The event would take place in the evening and would consist of recitations, songs and two plays. We were to invite our families and friends.

For the next month we learned to memorize our parts in the plays. About a week before the Christmas program, we spent our afternoons at the grange hall rehearsing on the stage. We walked the mile from school to the hall at lunchtime, eating our sandwiches on the way.

Ethel Rupert volunteered to play the piano to accompany our songs, which freed Mrs. Graham to direct the program and do the prompting for the plays. We had a one-act and a three-act play and had a lot of long lines to learn.

After much practice, the big night finally arrived. We were as ready as we'd ever be, and so was the beautiful Christmas tree which stood near the stage next to the built-in baby crib. Until I peeked through the curtains and saw the hall was full, I hadn't realized there would be such a big audience. All the benches lined up on the dance floor were filled, and there was standing room only in back.

Mrs. Graham welcomed everyone, and announced the first song. When it ended, the curtain closed and the audience clapped loudly. They liked everything we had to offer as we went through the entire program. At the end, Mrs. Graham came out from behind the curtains, asked us to join her on stage, and announced the program had ended. We bowed, and the audience clapped and clapped louder and stronger than before.

Just then sleigh bells jingled outside the front door. We turned to look, and there was Santa Claus coming through the door. For a minute, his red suit and white cotton beard made everything else in the hall fade away. Carrying a bulging sack over his shoulder, he strode past the audience, jolly and laughing his "Ho, ho, ho," and stopped by the tall Christmas tree near the stage. If I hadn't known better, I would have thought he was real.

Santa began calling the names of everyone in the Pleasant Valley School, and gave each a small paper sack of candy. But there was more to come. He also called the names of every child in the audience, and everyone under high school age received a sack of candy.

That was the best Christmas most of us could remember. It was also the beginning of a tradition. Mrs. Graham earned a reputation as a fine program director, and every year the grange hall was packed with people who came to have a good time — and perhaps see to it that their children had candy for Christmas. Life was hard for most of the folks; most were experiencing downright poverty.

A few years later, when Lester and I were in the seventh grade, the enrollment in school increased. A second teacher, Lawrence Hays, was hired, and both rooms in the little schoolhouse were in full use. Mrs. Graham continued teaching and had been named principal. Lawrence Hays wasn't a stranger in our valley. He owned the Hays Place we had once rented, and Hays Hill, where we enjoyed our winter fun, was named after him.

The following year, enrollment at the Arzina Grade School had dwindled, and the kids attended our school on a trial basis, bringing enrollment to forty-five pupils.

Ralph Byrd, who lived just inside the Arzina District, had switched to our school a couple of years before and was the only one who had a bicycle, which he rode to school. During recess I told him I wished I knew how to ride a bike.

"Come here, and I'll show you how," he answered. "Get on and hang onto the handlebars. When you want to stop, just push backward on the pedal," he instructed briefly.

I took off across the schoolyard and didn't slow down until I got to the other side near the barn. In the excitement, I had forgotten how to stop it. I yelled, "Whoa," like I did when riding a horse, and pulled on the handlebars. When that didn't work, I leaned to one side, tipping the bike over. Fortunately, I had slowed down enough and didn't hurt myself — or the borrowed bike.

Ralph was generous and let me ride his bike, and I finally learned how to stop properly instead of tipping over. It was fun, but it wasn't as good as riding a horse when going uphill. I wondered if Ralph wished he could borrow my horse when he had to push his bike up the steep Folsom Hill going home after school.

At the end of the trial year, the Arzina board members decided to consolidate with the Rice District, because its had three full classrooms and would be able to offer the Arzina pupils more in the long run.

Two or three times a year our school participated in track meets. When we met at Rice, only a few local schools were involved, but when we competed in the district track meet at Colville, all the schools in the county were represented.

Before our first track meet, we practiced for the events: the fifty-yard dash, one-hundred-yard dash, relay races, high jumping, broad jumping, running broad jumping, and pole vaulting. A pit was dug under the high-jump poles and filled with sawdust to make landing softer. I liked all the races best but discovered that I was pretty good at broad jumping, too. After trying to pole vault a few times, I gave it up because of the hard landings — the sawdust didn't help much to soften it. The track meets were a lot of fun. It was exciting to go places and win ribbons just like at our Fourth-of-July races at the grange hall.

At that particular meet we were getting ready for the standing broad jump contest to begin when, noticing my bare feet, one of the girls exclaimed, "You're not going to jump without tennis shoes, are you?"

"Oh, I can jump farther without them," I replied.

What I didn't tell her was that I didn't have tennis shoes. There just wasn't enough money to go around in our family. We owned only one pair of shoes at a time, and oxfords were more important than tennis shoes. My answer was partly right — I definitely could jump farther without my heavy oxfords. And after winning the blue ribbon, beating her and everyone else, she no longer looked scornfully at my bare feet. In spite of not having shorts or tennis shoes, our school won a lot of events. Most of us clutched blue, red and white ribbons on our way back to Pleasant Valley.

Sometimes we went on a picnic after the track meets. I tasted my first coconut cake after a track meet at Rice. The mothers of the participating kids spread tablecloths on the grass and brought out the food — sandwiches, pickles, deviled eggs and cakes. Ella Loven brought about two dozen lemons and squeezed them for lemonade. When it was time for dessert, a dazzling coconut cake caught my eye. With plenty of shredded coconut over thick white icing on the top and sides, and fluffy frosting between two white layers, it looked like snow on a mountain. It was delicious.

❧ ❧

In 1967, after all the Riley kids got through grade school, Pleasant Valley School District No. 32 was dissolved. Like the Arzina School, its enrollment had dwindled, and it wasn't long before the Rice School also closed. Buses took all the grade school and high school children to Kettle Falls.

The first school in Pleasant Valley was merely an empty room in a farmer's granary. In 1891, when Pleasant Valley School District No. 32 was established, there was no school building available, and Abe Wilkes offered the use of his granary. Soon afterward, the local farmers built a log schoolhouse a short distance from where Day Road branched off from Pleasant Valley Road.

In 1908, the Pleasant Valley School District built a two-room, frame schoolhouse — complete with belltower — across the road from the log school. The new building remained unpainted for a few years before getting its first coat of white paint, and it remained in use for fifty-eight years.

Lawrence Hays bought the two-room school building and tore it down for its lumber. But the bell and its belltower went to Paul Holter, who had served as a school board member for many years.

16

Coulee Dam Under Construction

Mrs. Graham, our teacher, was full of surprises. After establishing the tradition of Christmas programs at the grange hall, she took us on a bus ride more than a hundred miles to see a dam being built at Grand Coulee. Promising it would be an educational outing, she also told us that it would be something we would long remember.

Mrs. Graham said that in 1933, President Franklin D. Roosevelt had authorized funds for the dam to be built under his Public Works Administration program. She went on to say that the dam would irrigate hundreds of acres of desert land around Moses Lake and Pasco in the Columbia Basin. Besides turning useless land into producing farmland, the dam would furnish additional electric power for industries which would create jobs during the Depression.

After obtaining the school board's permission for the two-day trip, Mrs. Graham announced we would depart the first week in June, right after school was out. She rented a bus, lined up a volunteer bus driver and several parents to go along to help. She also reserved several tourist cabins in Soap Lake, where we would stop overnight. I was glad when Mom told us she had volunteered to go along, while Dad took care of the little girls at home.

Going on to Soap Lake, which was south of Coulee Dam, added extra miles to our trip, but Mrs. Graham thought the "unique quality" of the lake made the detour worthwhile. Not understanding what she meant, I had to wait until we got there to find out.

We started out early, in the cool of the morning. Before getting to Davenport, we could tell it was going to be a hot day. By afternoon, when we were in the desert area east of Soap Lake, we had opened most of the bus windows to let the hot wind blow in our faces. But that didn't help much. All we could think of was getting to that cool lake so we could go swimming.

The week before the trip, Mom had taken me to Colville to buy me a bathing suit because I had outgrown mine. None of the bathing suits at J.C. Penney fit right, and Mom astounded me by saying, "Let's go across the street to Barman's and see if we can find one that fits."

I was shocked. Barman's was a fancy store with expensive merchandise, and we rarely went there. There were several suits available in my size, but I loved a bright orange two-piece suit best. It felt good when I put it on, and the mirror told me that it looked good, too. When Mom said we could buy it, I was overjoyed.

Nearing the town of Soap Lake brought me closer to wearing my new bathing suit. The bus stopped at the cabins so we could change into our suits. We got back on the bus for the short drive to the lake. When we arrived, we made a screaming dash for the clear water and jumped in, splashing water in our mouths. Surprise! The water tasted terrible, just like the times Mom made me wash my mouth out with soap when I'd said some cuss words. It became quite clear what Mrs. Graham meant by the "unique quality" of the lake.

Despite all the minerals, the water was just as clear as the Columbia River. My orange bathing suit glistened as I flashed through the water doing the sidestroke. When a couple of boys swam by doing the crawl, I tried to copy them but wound up splashing more of that soapy-tasting water into my mouth. I decided it was more fun to flip over onto my back and float and watch the clouds sailing by in the bright blue summer sky.

The long bus ride and our swim had tired us out, and everyone was only too glad to go to bed early that night. Our group of more than forty filled quite a few cabins, but we still had to double up. I shared a sagging double bed with another girl, who wet the bed during the night and tried to convince Mrs. Graham that I was the guilty one. But our teacher wasn't fooled easily. She noticed it wasn't my nightgown that was wet. My respect for her increased when she didn't even bother to ask me about it.

After breakfast we headed north to see Coulee Dam. When we arrived, it was hard to imagine what exactly was being built in all the noise and confusion and dust. Jackhammer workers clung to rocky cliffs, drilling holes for dynamite, while other workers swarmed over a high framework of scaffolding.

It looked like dangerous work. While we watched, all work stopped in one area so the powder monkeys could set off dynamite to blast off the face of a rocky cliff. When the charge went off, a huge section of cliff disappeared in a cloud of dust and flying rocks. After it fell, the sound of the blast reached us — it was the loudest noise I'd ever heard. After several minutes, the dust cleared and we could see the big scar on the rock face. We watched the activity for a couple of hours before turning around and heading back toward the quiet and peaceful life at Pleasant Valley.

❧ ❧

Building the dam *was* dangerous. Before it was finished in 1941, several construction men died in accidents. They were so desperate for any kind of work during the Depression, they willingly risked their lives just to be making some money.

17

Dad's Gunshot Wound

The grazing land and thickets of brush on the wooded hills of our isolated farm were home to game. Coyotes came in to steal our chickens, but we rarely saw them. At night the coyotes howled, reminding us to keep the chicken-house door shut. Much of the pastureland was on hills too steep or rocky for farming, and in the spring the grass grew undisturbed by plow or mowing machine. Deer sometimes grazed alongside the cattle, their narrow, pointed hoofprints mingling with the bigger and deeper impressions the cattle left behind. Dad was more interested in deer than the coyotes.

Lured by sprouting hay and grain, the deer came down from Monumental Mountain, a mile or two east of us, to eat the fresh, tender shoots. We found tracks of all sizes, from the small ones of the fawns to the big ones of old bucks. When we saw them crossing the newly plowed and harrowed fields, we could easily follow their tracks until they crossed onto the harder ground of the pasture. We liked tracing the firm impressions with our fingers, feeling the smoothness and knowing a deer had stood there.

Each year we raised a few calves and lambs but couldn't afford to kill them for our own use. We sold them to get a little money to buy the things we couldn't raise — like sugar, clothing, gas and tires. Money was scarce for all farmers during the Great Depression. We never had a dollar to spare and came as close to living off the land as anyone. We relied almost totally on the deer for our meat supply.

When we needed food for the table, Dad picked up his thirty-thirty lever-action Winchester rifle from a corner in the kitchen and went hunting. He also carried a pistol in his homemade shoulder holster, which he used for the killing shot on the deer he hadn't killed outright with the rifle. (Pistol bullets cost less than rifle bullets.)

He could usually find a deer on the far side of our farm but occasionally had to hike as far away as Monumental Mountain. Sometimes he drove over to the Arzina area to hunt with his favorite hunting partners, Pearl Entwistle and Bill Preston, in the mountainous areas near their farms.

Dad was a good hunter and usually got his deer. But there was one time when he shot himself instead of a deer. Having separated from his hunting buddies, he bent over to roll a boulder down into the brush to scare a deer out into the open. His pistol fell out of the holster, dropped butt first onto the boulder and discharged. The bullet tore through Dad's flesh below his left armpit. He felt under his arm, and when he saw the warm blood coating his hand, he passed out cold.

Bill Preston and Pearl were close enough to hear the pistol shot and came running, expecting to see Dad standing over a dead deer. Alarmed, they bent over the still figure on the ground and noticed he was still breathing. In propping him up, Bill Preston's hand got wet with blood. That's when they realized Dad had been shot. About that time, to the immense relief of his friends, Dad opened his eyes. What they didn't know was the fact that he couldn't stand the sight of his own blood and had promptly passed out.

Blood was seeping from a bullet wound on the left side of his chest near his armpit. When the men rolled him a little to one side, they discovered blood oozing out of a hole where the bullet had exited.

Bill Preston took his shirt off, folded it into a thick pad, and put it over the bullet holes, applying pressure to stop the bleeding, and tied a piece of binding twine around Dad's chest to keep the bandage in place. His friends helped him to his feet and, supporting him on each side, they led him down the mountain to the car. Pearl drove as fast as he could to our place to pick up Mom so she could go to Colville with them.

When Lester, Dora and I got home from school, we were shocked to find Dad in bed. We had never seen our father in bed during the daytime. His face was ash-colored and he looked so weak we were almost afraid to talk to him. Mom told us that he had been shot and assured us he was going be all right.

She explained how Dad had gotten hurt and how Pearl had taken him to the doctor, ending up with, "He's lucky the bullet didn't go in a couple more inches to the left and hit his heart. Now you understand why we tell you to always be careful with guns."

It didn't take Dad long to recover from his wound. The bullet holes healed, leaving two round, shiny-white, smooth scars. For years afterward whenever we saw him with his shirt off, we stared in curious fascination at the reminders of his hunting accident, realizing how lucky he was not to have been killed. We saw for ourselves what a bullet could do to a person, as well as to a deer.

Dad seemed to feel a little sheepish about shooting himself and passing out. And although he and his friends kidded each other almost every chance they got, I never once heard Pearl or Bill Preston razz him about this. I thought maybe it was because it was too serious a matter.

❖   ❖

In a recent letter from Goldie Entwistle, she recalls this incident. "They took him over to your folks' place and Audrey went with them to the doctor. When they got back from town, they were still talking about Bill getting so sick when he saw he was losing blood."

18

Hunting Lessons

When Dad had first started taking me hunting, I was only eight years old and thrilled to to go with him. He had been taking Lester for a couple of years, and I wanted to learn how to hunt, too.

His main reason for taking us wasn't as much as to teach us about hunting, but to do the "driving" for him. Our job as drivers was to go through the brush making a lot of noise to scare the deer out into the open so he could get a shot at them. Dad would find the spot where he knew the deer would pass by — and send us through the thickets to chase them out. He knew from past hunts which direction they ran, and he knew where the best spots were.

One morning, after taking us into the timber below the house and telling us when we should start our drive, Dad had left us to get to his stand. Lester and I talked in whispers while we waited. But when we began the drive, we made a lot of noise, called back and forth to each other, and whacked the bushes and trees with sticks.

We heard the boom of Dad's gun, followed by a second shot. To be sure Dad was through shooting, we waited in order not to get into his line of fire. My mouth watered after I thought about how good the heart and liver were going to taste. We were tired and ready to go home — tramping across the hills through the brush was hard work.

Coming out of the thicket into the open area, we looked around. Like so many times before, we found our father squatting beside a dead deer, sharpening his jackknife on a little round whetstone. The round outline of that whetstone marked the bib pocket of every one of his overalls.

Perhaps he thought it was bad luck to sharpen his knife before the hunt, since he always waited with that chore until after he killed his deer. But we knew it took more than luck. Dad was a good shot with a rifle and never missed if he had a clear shot. One thing puzzled me about his shooting — he shot left-handed but did everything else right-handed.

Dad would aim just behind the deer's shoulder, intending to hit the heart and avoid tearing up a lot of meat. A bullet in the stomach or in the intestines made the deer so dirty it was almost impossible to clean. A good hunter would be ashamed to have gut-shot a deer.

By the time Dad had told us all this, he had finished sharpening his knife and was ready to start gutting the deer. We held the deer's legs out of his way as he quickly finished the job.

We learned that there was a lot more to hunting than just shooting at deer. Dad taught us to look for tracks, and explained how deer made a different kind of track running than walking. He'd point to a great big deer track where the two parts of the hoof were spread wide and say, "Now here's a big buck, and he's running to beat hell!"

He showed us the difference between a yearling's tracks and those of a full-grown deer. Seeing some medium-size, evenly spaced tracks, Dad said, "This is a yearling deer just moseying along." As the tracks suddenly became spaced farther apart, the narrow points dug into the dirt, he added, "Here's where it was spooked and lit out running."

Lester and I became so fascinated with deer tracks that we watched for them when we weren't hunting, and kept looking at the ground whether we were walking or riding our horse. On our way home from school, we taught Dora what we had learned.

Once we spotted bear tracks, and I had a scary feeling that the owner of these tracks might be just behind the thicket, watching us. Lester's horse had shied, and that could mean the bear's scent was on the wind. Kicking Betty into a gallop, I yelled, "Hang on, Dora," and off we went, hightailing after Lester to the safety of the barn.

On another hunting trip, we came upon some deer beds in the tall grass. Lester and I put the palms of our hands down where the deer had lain, surprised that the ground was still warm. Dad looked at the flattened-down grass, and at the scattered dark brown, oval droppings which were still steaming in the cool air. "Several deer spent the night here," he said, "and they've just left. Look for tracks to see which way they headed." We circled the beds and found tracks that led uphill. Dad took one look at them and said, "They went up the mountain when they heard us coming."

Our father also taught us to look for landmarks when we were in strange territory so that we always could find our way home — anything from a rock jutting out from a hill, a rockslide, a stand of pines, a swamp, or anything else that stuck out and looked different.

On one of my first drives, when I was eight, I had lost sight of Lester and Dad because I had gone a bit astray. Misjudging my route through the thick brush, I veered too far into the wrong direction. Instead of going straight across the slope, I gradually climbed uphill. About fifteen minutes later I came out into the open, but I couldn't see Lester anywhere, and I did get a little worried. Enough time had passed for them to have reached our meeting place. Remembering how Dad had described the spot, I tried to pick it out.

Standing on the high point, I looked long and hard. Finally, on a hillside far below me, looking so small I could just barely make them out, I spotted my hunting companions. Feeling very much alone and scared, I was glad to have located them. They were so far away that I wasn't sure they could hear me, but I cupped my hands around my mouth and I yelled as loud as I could, "Dad, I'm up here. Wait for me."

He heard me, and yelled back, "Come on down here."

With so much rough country separating us and no trail leading in that direction, I couldn't see an easy way of getting there. Feeling a little silly, I yelled, "How am I going to get there?"

Dad yelled back, "Fly!"

I knew I'd never forget Dad's laughing reply and really felt foolish. I headed down the slope, and twenty minutes later I sank gratefully to the ground beside him. He never teased me about getting lost.

Long before we were old enough to shoot, Dad had us help him clean and oil the rifles, which always stood fully loaded in a corner behind the kitchen door. He was of the opinion that a rifle wasn't any good unless it was loaded. We were trained from babyhood that guns weren't playthings and learned early in life to take care of them.

I was surprised to find working the lever-action so enjoyable. Its oiled metallic sound was pleasurable and, with my right hand gripping the lever, I could feel a silkiness in the smooth-working action. We handed the rifles to Dad to reload, giving him the shells out of our pockets. Cleaning the rifles and carrying them home after a hunt, we became familiar and comfortable with them long before we were allowed to use them. Our father's lessons had sunk in — none of us ever got truly lost in the woods or had a hunting accident.

⊰≫ ⊰≪⊱

Although I was never much of a deer hunter, Dad's hunting lessons gave me a lifelong love of the hills and mountains. And more than fifty years since he told me not to point a gun at anyone, I cringe if anyone points even a toy pistol at me.

19

Going Places
in the Star

We were riding in our old Star — the very same car that had brought us from Oregon to our new home. Good for rough country roads, the car sat high off the ground and could straddle rocks and the high furrows of ruts without scraping bottom. The running boards were a long step up for little kids, but by the time I was ten, they didn't seem so high.

As the car bounced down the narrow dirt road of Heidegger Hill, the wheels kicked up loose rocks that rattled against the floorboards. Wind rushing through the car made it seem like we were going faster than twenty miles an hour. From where I sat, I had a good view of the drop-off into the bottom of the small canyon. I fervently hoped we wouldn't meet a car coming uphill, because the solid rock wall on the left and a drop-off on the right didn't leave much room for passing. The worst spot was a corner where the road was a solid sheet of rock that tipped on a slant toward the canyon. Without a guard rail between the edge of the road and the drop-off made it a scary place.

Dad gripped the big steering wheel with both hands, making sure we stayed in the middle of the road. I thought he was so big and strong and smart to be able to drive a car. Mom sat beside him holding Effie; Lester and I sat by the windows, with Dora and Leola squished in the middle.

We were headed for Colville, over thirty miles away, and only a small part of that distance took place on a paved highway. The town was the county seat of Stevens County and the main shopping area for many miles around. We were getting new shoes before school started, and Mom needed a few things, too. For us children it was a real outing, a break from everyday routine, and presented us with its own brand of adventure. The only time we got to go to town was when we had to try on shoes or clothing for a good fit.

Colville, with a population of over 2,500, was the biggest town in our area and prided itself on having several solid-looking brick buildings. The cream-colored courthouse sat back against a wide lawn shaded by tall trees. Scattered through the town were a hospital, a post office, banks, public library, two department stores — Barman's and J.C. Penney's — a Greyhound bus depot, restaurants, a dime store and hardware store, a few taverns and a weekly newspaper, *The Statesman's Index*. The county fairgrounds, with a grandstand, horseracing track and exhibit barns, were down a hill near the flour mill.

In addition to our school shoes, Mom had to get cotton stockings for herself and us girls, long woolen underwear for all of us and fabric for dresses. Dad and Lester joined us at Penney's shoe department, where Dora and I tried on sturdy oxfords, while Lester was looking at work shoes that reached above his ankles. Dad would push down on the tips of our shoes with his fingers to make sure there was enough room to grow because our shoes had to last until school was out the following spring.

After buying at the grocery store the things we couldn't raise on the farm — like oatmeal, wheat flakes, farina, sugar, rice, macaroni, cheese, peanut butter, Karo syrup (in half-gallon cans with bails), raisins, soap and a few other items, we were finished with shopping. We didn't have to buy flour. Once a year Dad took some of our wheat to the flour mill and traded for enough flour to last a year. We seldom bought meat because of all the deer Dad killed and the pig and the few sheep he butchered. We kept our steers to sell.

While we were getting groceries, Dad bought ammunition for his deer rifles and the twenty-twos, and a paper bag of hoarhound drops — a favorite treat that didn't cost much money.

Another treat was having a sandwich for lunch at Old King Cole's Restaurant, rather than stopping alongside the road on our way home to make our own lunch. As soon as we got seated, Leola and Effie spotted a couple of dimes and a nickel on the table among the clutter of dirty dishes. Eagerly picking up the coins, Leola exclaimed, "Look, Mom, we found some money." When the waitress came to clear the table, we wondered why she had a frown on her face. We didn't realize that the loose change had been left for her. As soon as we finished our lunch, we headed back to the farm, sucking on our hard hoarhound candy. It would be a long ride home, and the evening chores were waiting for us.

Frequent snowstorms and freezing weather limited town trips to just a few outings. Driving a car then was a lot more difficult on our icy, narrow country roads. Getting the Star ready to travel in the winter was also hard work, but it didn't take quite as much time as plowing out the road. Dad had to put the chains on the back wheels, fill the radiator, and turn the crank until the engine started. The chains had so much wear that several of the links would break, clanking against the fender, making a continuous metallic whap-whap, and had to be wired to the main chain.

Just to start the car winter or summer was an event. Dad set the brake, shifted into neutral, pulled out the choke, and carefully set the spark and gas lever. If the spark came too soon, it would cause the crank to kick backwards and could break a man's arm. Then he took the crank and stuck the end of the crank into the hole just below the radiator. With a strong right-handed motion, he turned the crank until the engine started. He quickly removed the crank and ran back to the driver's seat to adjust the choke and another lever to slow down the racing engine. When the engine stopped spluttering and purred smoothly, he put the crank back under the seat.

About the only place we went by car in the winter was to Colville or the Quillisascut Grange Hall. When we had to go all the way to Colville, Mom heated up two or three flatirons to help keep our feet warm and took a quilt along. Hunched up under the quilt and shivering with cold, I wished we could put a stove in the car, but I couldn't figure out a way. When we got to our destination, we covered the hood of the car with an old quilt to keep the water in the radiator from freezing.

Because of all the time and effort involved in winter driving, we didn't go anywhere in the car unless we had a special reason. That was fine with me. Going down the steep, slippery, snow-covered Heidegger Hill didn't appeal to me anyway. We hadn't heard of cars sliding off the road into the canyon, but I didn't want ours to be the first one.

20

Trapping

Extra money was hard to come by during the Depression, and people looked every which way to earn a few extra dollars. Trapping animals and selling their pelts to fur buyers in Spokane became a small source of income for us. During the winter, when pelts were at their best, Dad set his trap lines, some of which extended into Frank Rupert's farm. Since Frank didn't want coyotes to be killing his newborn calves but couldn't do trapping himself, he was glad to let Dad set traps on his land. Dad once pulled one of his practical jokes on Frank's visiting grandsons, who asked him if coyotes made good eating. The boys had come upon him while he was skinning two of those predators that had been caught in his trap. Convincing them that hindquarters made good steaks and other parts were great for mulligan stew, the boys gladly took the offering of the rear end of a coyote, while Dad took the pelts home. Frank and Dad often told the story and chuckled over it for years.

There were plenty of coyotes in our part of the country, and we listened to their howling and yip-yipping night after night. Dad also trapped muskrats and occasional mink, and we all got involved in helping him.

As the oldest girl of five children, I had household chores to do before helping my father outside or following him around on his trapline. When Lester went with him to check his traps, I wanted to go, too. I was ten years old and still a tomboy at heart. I hurried washing the breakfast dishes and sweeping the kitchen floor, so I would be ready when they were.

We watched Dad set a coyote trap by scooping out a depression in the center of the animal trail, he set the trap and placed it in the low spot he'd made. Picking up the chain attached to the trap, he fastened it to a log. "If there isn't a log or a tree near where I want to put the trap, I drive a strong stake into the ground and fasten the chain to it. If the chain isn't fastened to something solid, the coyote will just run off, dragging the trap with him. Then we'll be out the trap and the pelt, too," he explained.

From a small bottle of dark liquid that smelled like rotten eggs, he sprinkled a few drops on the trap to cover up the "man-scent." After getting a whiff of the vile-smelling stuff, Lester and I knew why the coyote wouldn't be able to smell either the iron trap or man's scent on it. We couldn't smell anything for a while either. For a final touch, Dad placed a few small sticks and dry leaves across the trap, being careful not to spring it.

We could always tell when Dad had been out setting traps. We could smell that awful scent that stayed with him. Even our strong lye soap didn't get it off the first time he washed himself. A few times he got careless and spilled that stuff on his overalls! Then

Mom scolded, "Bill, you'll have to be more careful with that scent."
Mom's wash day was hard enough without having to smell rotten
eggs while she scrubbed clothes.

Most of the animals he caught were muskrats, but a few mink
and coyotes got into his traps, too. The mink pelts brought the most
money, coyotes the least. But some years the government paid a
five-dollar bounty for each coyote, which helped make up for the
little bit of money paid for their pelts. We checked the trapline
about every other day. When an animal had been caught, Dad
removed it, reset the trap, sprinkled a few drops of scent on it, and
concealed it again.

The way Dad skinned a muskrat reminded me of the way I
pulled a sweater off over my head. Using his sharp jackknife, he
started by cutting clear through each leg bone right above the paw,
while leaving it attached to the hide. He then hung the muskrat up
by its hind legs upside down, so it was easier to work on. He
continued by cutting the skin across the back end of the body,
making a long cut from one hind leg over to the other, which
enabled him to pull the hide down all around the body, while
cutting the thin tissue between the hide and body. When he finished,
the hide was whole, but wrong-side out. It looked like its owner had
pulled it off over its head — just as I did my sweater — and walked
off, leaving it behind.

Dad had built several wooden stretchers to fit the animals'
hides for drying, which took about three weeks. He was taking
some muskrat pelts off the stretchers one afternoon just as we got
home from school, and I was eager to help.

After I washed my hands, Dad handed me a muskrat pelt
ready to be taken off the stretcher. Holding onto the white rawhide
pelt with one hand, I pulled the wooden stretcher out with the other.
Although the pelt was stiff enough to stand by itself, it was still
pliable. I turned the pelt right side out, pulling the hind part down

over the head. Once again, the whole glossy, dark brown fur was on the outside, looking so alive.

I stroked the pelt from head to tail, feeling the softness and admiring its beauty. This had to be the best part about trapping! Next, I worked on a mink, smaller than the muskrat and even more beautiful and luxurious —the glossy fur was so dark it was almost black. My fingers sank into the silky softness of this glistening fur. I tried to picture the rich lady who'd be wearing a coat made from mink pelts. During these hard times, when we bought one pair of shoes just once a year, it was hard to imagine someone rich enough to buy an expensive mink coat.

Of all the time Dad spent working his trapline, the day he pulled the joke on Frank by sending him some fresh coyote meat for supper was the most fun. A few years later Frank got even with him. Part of his hillside had slid down, crossed the county road, and ended up in our field — the trees still standing upright. "Bill," he said laughing hugely, "I want you to bring my land back and put it up on the bank where it belongs. That will teach you to send coyote steaks to me!"

The men kept the stories going for years. Trapping had indeed become part of our activities, but no matter how many chicken-stealing varmints Dad caught in his traps, there were still plenty of coyotes that howled at night.

21

Wash Day

"Lester and Ines, you two get busy and start carrying water to fill the tubs and the boiler. We have to wash today, and I want to get started early." Mom gave us our marching orders on washday.

We all knew wash day meant a long hard day's work. Lester and I each grabbed two ten-quart galvanized milk buckets and set out for the well about a hundred yards from the house. We heard a clanking behind us and turned to see eight-year-old Dora running and swinging a bucket in her hand.

At thirteen and eleven, Lester and I were strong enough to carry a full bucket of water in each hand. This wasn't much work, except for wash day and our Saturday-night baths, which, for the seven of us, meant extra trips to the well. It also meant everyone big enough to work had to do something. Even four-year-old Leola helped by keeping an eye on Effie and playing with her.

Lester untied the well-bucket's rope from the framework above the well and let the bucket drop. It splashed when it hit the water. The rope holding the bucket ran through a pulley above the well, which made it easier hauling the buckets of water out of the well. When we carried our full buckets into the kitchen, Mom had a good hot fire going in the cookstove to heat the water fast so she could finish scrubbing clothes before noon, when the day got to be too hot.

In summer, we set up the washtubs on benches in the yard and scrubbed clothes on the washboard under the blue sky. It didn't matter if we splashed water out of the tubs onto the grass. When we washed in the kitchen, we always had to mop the linoleum floor after finishing with the wash. It was also cooler scrubbing clothes away from the hot cookstove — if we could finish before the sun got too hot. In the winter, we had to do the washing in the kitchen.

We made several trips to the well. Filling the round-ended wash boiler and the two round zinc washtubs took a lot of water. When the rinse water in the tubs got soapy, Mom dumped it out on the ground. We had to make more trips to the well, carrying enough water to refill the tubs, as well as keeping the woodbox filled with firewood.

When Mom finished sorting the clothes, she put some of the white clothes into the boiler and boiled them, shaving some soap curls from a bar of yellow Fels Naptha into the boiler full of clothes. After the first batch of clothes had boiled for a few minutes, Mom lifted them out piece by piece with her long clothes stick (which she had made by peeling the bark off of a green tree branch), put them into the washtub, and refilled the boiler with a second batch of white clothes. Now the hard work started. She took the washboard down from the wall and started scrubbing.

Mom scrubbed until her arms got tired, then I took over. I had started helping Mom scrub on the board when I was about nine.

When I was eleven years old, I felt like an old hand and could scrub clothes on the washboard for ten or fifteen minutes before my arms gave out.

Each piece had to be wrung out by hand, tossed into the first tub of rinse water, and then we continued washing all the clothes in the tub. Finishing with washing that batch of clothes, we rinsed them in two tubs of water. After swishing them around in the first tub to get the soap out, we ran them through the wringer into the other tub of rinse water.

One person turned the handle of the wringer, which was clamped onto the edge of the washtub, while another person fed the clothes through the rollers of the wringer. Lester, Dora and I took turns doing this while Mom was taking more clothes out of the wash boiler on the stove. We rinsed the clothes for the second time and ran them through the wringer, this time letting them fall into a large dishpan. They were finally ready to be hung on the clothesline to dry.

After finishing the last pile of dirty overalls and hanging them up, we still weren't through with our wash day jobs. We had to empty the water from the boiler and tubs, wash them and hang them up and mop the kitchen floor. We had to take the clothes off the line when they had dried, fold and put away the flat pieces, and set aside those that needed ironing.

Wash day was real drudgery, and we were all dead tired when it was over. There wasn't an easier way to do it, because we didn't have the money to buy a gasoline-powered washing machine.

Ironing the clothes wasn't as big a job as washing them, but it wasn't any fun, either. Mom rested up for a day or two before tackling another tiring job. She did it all by herself until I was ten, when I started ironing the small pieces. When I graduated to ironing workshirts and dresses, I found it hard to get the wrinkles out without making more wrinkles.

Between us, we could finish the basket of ironing in about three hours. Even though we took turns, it seemed like we'd never get done. It was worse on a hot day, as the kitchen got unbearably stuffy because we had to keep the fire in the stove going to heat the irons.

None of us enjoyed wash day or ironing day. But all the hard work we did made us kids appreciate our free time, and we felt happy and carefree when we got out to roam and explore.

22

"Doctor" Mom

In the summertime, Lester, Dora and I spent most of our time outdoors and had many painful encounters with yellow jackets, hornets, thorns, barbed-wire fences, stickers, brambles and boards with rusty nails. Mom wound up taking care of our cuts, bruises, bee stings and all the other hurts. Although her remedies sometimes stung worse than the injury, we went to her for help.

She used her own brand of medicine, some of which she had adopted by trial and error, and others had originated with her mother. Her favorite remedy was turpentine which she used on scratches and deep skin punctures. She put iodine or Mercurochrome on minor cuts, liniment on bruises, and a baking soda paste on bee stings. When we had colds, she relied on Vicks' VapoRub and applied mustard plasters to our chests. For chapped hands, she rubbed on Bag Balm, an antiseptic salve Dad used on the cows' teats when they became cracked. He had accidentally discovered its healing ability when he had a cut on his finger. The following day, after putting the salve on the cow's teat, his cut was healed. Mom immediately added Bag Balm to her list of remedies.

When we tangled with yellow jackets, she made a paste of baking soda and water and applied it to the spot where we'd been stung. Those nasty flying stingers lit on the rotting fruit under the apple and pear trees, making it almost impossible to pick fruit without getting stung. We either stepped on the bees accidentally or they attacked us when we climbed the trees. That's when we high-tailed it for home and Mom's soda paste.

There were a lot of yellow jacket nests in the woods, but once we found a nest right in the wall of our house. Every time Mom walked out to the garden, these menaces buzzed threateningly around her head, so she told us to find their nest. We tiptoed around the house, checking the boards near the corners, and noticed yellow jackets darting in and out of a hole in the side of the house. Located in the empty space between the outside and inside walls, this was one nest we couldn't knock down. When we reported our find to Mom, she said, "Never mind. One of these days your father will think of a way to get rid of them."

Until the day unexpected visitors arrived, we steered clear of that corner of the house. Not many people came to see us, since we weren't easy to reach by road and didn't have a telephone. That's why we were pleasantly surprised when a carful of people chugged up the wagon road and stopped in front of the house.

Lester and I were eager to tell our visitors all about the yellow jackets nesting in the side of the house, and during a lull in the grownups' conversation, we launched into our story. Volunteering to show our visitors our discovery, I led them around the corner. Unknown to me, Lester went inside the house to do his part. Just as we reached the spot with the hole, Lester pounded on the inside wall.

The yellow jackets swarmed crazily out of the hole and attacked us, buzzing angrily around our heads and nailing us with their stingers. Mom heard our alarming yells and hurried into the kitchen to make up some soda paste. I'd been stung so many times, I'd broken out in welts and red spots all over my body. Dabbing the white paste on some of the stings on my arm, Mom soon realized she would have to use a different remedy and decided to give me a soda-water bath.

We set one of the zinc wash tubs in the yard, filled it with lukewarm water, dumped a whole box of baking soda in, and stirred it with a stick. Before the soda dissolved, I had my clothes off and was in the tub. I didn't care if our visitors did see me naked— I'd do anything to stop the pain of the stings.

The soda bath worked; soon the welts disappeared and the stings stopped hurting. And Mom was right about Dad — he found a way to get rid of the yellow jackets by spraying poison into the hole where they nested. The next morning there was no sign of them. He nailed a board over the hole to discourage other swarms from moving in.

The bee stings were an annoyance but weren't nearly as dangerous as the rusty nails our bare feet seemed to attract. I once stepped on a short board with a nail sticking straight up. The nail went so far into my foot that when I started to walk, the board lifted off the ground. With the board still nailed to my foot, I hopped to the house to find Mom. Unlike me, she wasn't squeamish; she grasped the board and pulled it off. After soaking my foot in hot boric-acid water, Mom poured turpentine over it, making sure some of it went up into the nail hole. The turpentine stung so bad it made me cry — which I hadn't done when I stepped on the nail.

But the cure was effective. The wound healed, and I didn't get lockjaw or blood poisoning. It was a wonder — none of us had ever gone to a doctor for tetanus shots.

While nails caused our most serious injuries, they didn't keep Mom as busy as our less-serious injuries. She kept a sharp needle handy for removing slivers from our fingers we picked up from carrying in wood. We couldn't walk through brush without getting thorns stuck on some parts of our bodies. We didn't like it when Mom had to probe around with the needle and often wouldn't tell her about the thorns and stickers hiding under the skin until they started to fester. Then she dug them out and poured turpentine on the sores.

She put liniment on the bruises Dora and I got the last time Dad spanked us. At eight and eleven, we knew better than to swing on the clothesline, and we were just running back and forth holding onto the lines. All of a sudden we saw Dad coming across the wheat stubble toward the house. We knew he'd think we had been swinging on the clothesline, were afraid to face him, and ran and hid — Dora in a closet and I in the cellar. He found us in our separate hiding places and gave us each a hard spanking. I was lying on the bed crying when Mom came in to rub her healing liniment all over my aching back and rear end. I sobbed, "But we weren't swinging on the clothesline at all."

She said, "He knew that; he spanked you because you ran and hid from him."

Mom took good care of us when we had measles and chicken pox. She kept the window shades pulled down to "protect" our eyes, and made us stay in bed longer than we liked. She wouldn't even let us go out to the toilet, but brought us her chamber pot.

We were like a lot of other people who lived a long way from the nearest doctor. People just didn't see a doctor or go to the hospital unless they had pneumonia, broken bones, or were going to have a baby. Mom was the only one in our family who had ever gone to a doctor.

In the winter when we had bad colds and coughed a lot, she rubbed Vicks' VapoRub on our chests before sending us to bed. And many times during the night we woke up to find her bending over us, applying another layer of the medicated rub. When we had whooping cough, she used a mustard plaster, which she made by mixing flour and dry mustard with hot water into a gooey paste. After putting the mixture between two pieces of cloth, she applied the mustard plaster on our chests for about fifteen minutes. She was careful not to use too much mustard in the mix or leave it on too long because it could burn our skin.

We didn't care for our father's remedies for colds and sore throats. One was kerosene, which he poured from the lantern onto a spoon, added a bit of sugar, and handed it to the one with a cold, saying, "Coal oil is what I took for a cold when I was little. Drink it; it will be good for your throat." It was awful!

His other remedy consisted of pouring a tablespoon of his own moonshine whiskey into a cup of hot water with a teaspoon of sugar. The hot toddy tasted a whole lot better than his dose of kerosene, and we would gladly have taken a second helping had it been offered.

Since Mom had never given us either of these remedies; we thought she probably didn't approve of them. When Effie almost choked trying to swallow Dad's prescribed spoonful of kerosene, Mom declared with conviction, "That's enough. That's the last time we'll take kerosene for medicine."

She rarely crossed Dad, but we were glad she stood up to him that time.

We didn't keep track of all our childhood diseases, or how many times we ran into barbed-wire fences with our sleds, stepped on nails, got stung, fell off or got bucked off the horses and fell out of trees. Despite it all, no one one ever broke bones, and we were never hurt so badly that Doctor Mom couldn't cure us.

23

Fourth-of-July
Celebration - 1935

Each year we looked forward to the Fourth-of-July celebration at the Quillisascut Grange Hall with great anticipation. Our parents wouldn't think of missing the festivities on the most exciting day of summer — it was all we talked about for days.

Besides having a chance to win some money in the footraces, we would see friends we hadn't seen since school let out. Our closest pals lived across the hills more than two miles away, and if we wanted to see them, we had to walk. Because our friends were as isolated from the world as we were, the Fourth-of-July celebration was a special day for them as well.

Dora and I were having our hair wound up in rag curlers so we could have curly hair for the big day, which meant suffering through a lot of tugs and pulls as Mom wrapped wet strands of hair around white strips of cloth. We talked about how much fun we had

had the previous year's festivities and how much money we had won in the footraces. Mom, who seldom left the farm, was looking forward to the outing even more than we were; she, too, longed to see her friends again.

The Fourth of July also meant having those wonderful things like ice cream cones, soda pop and firecrackers. But in order to be able to buy all those special treats, we had to win the prize money, which consisted of nickels, dimes and quarters. It was the only money we could ever spend recklessly.

The day-long celebration was for everyone — and more than a hundred people attended, who had to drive miles to get there. People helped with the program, the races, or worked in the booths; and others, like Mom, who had to watch over two little girls, came just to share in the holiday fun and visit with friends and neighbors. Grown-ups probably considered the main events of the day to be the big picnic under the shade trees and the short program in the hall, which usually consisted of a couple of speeches, some patriotic songs, and a performance by the grange's drill team.

Our heads were full of all the fun we expected to have. But before we could go, we still had to complete a big chore: we had to shock a late cutting of hay, which was unusual for that time of year. Several days of rain in June had kept Dad from mowing, and he had to rake the hay into windrows and left to dry thoroughly. Since he was busy with other chores, Mom, Lester, Dora and I had to shock the hay. My big brother, at thirteen, was strong and could shock hay almost as fast as his father.

Taking our pitchforks and a gallon jug of drinking water, the six of us headed to the hayfield. Effie and Leola went along, although they were too little to help, and still had to be watched. The blazing sun soon burned off the morning's coolness, and sweat ran down our foreheads as we pulled the loose green hay from the windrows with our pitchforks and piled it in individual shocks.

Dust and small bits of hay settled on us and got down our necks, making us feel itchy. We didn't enjoy working in the hot sun — but it was a perfect day for drying thick hair wound up in rag curlers.

After finishing shocking the hay that afternoon, we were hot, dirty and dusty, and ready to take our baths. Lester and I made several trips to the well, each carrying two buckets of water at a time. While the water heated in the copper-bottomed wash boiler on top of the cookstove, Mom beat up the ingredients for a cake to take to the picnic. By the time she had it all put together, the oven had heated to the right temperature, and the cake baked while we bathed.

We were almost ready for the next day's celebration.

The big day finally arrived. The Fourth-of-July celebration was more important to us than Christmas. Our curls were tight and firm from baking in the sun all day while we shocked hay. We put on dresses instead of bib overalls, and Lester put on his newest overalls and shirt. Mom looked nice in her best cotton house dress, and Dad, having worn nothing but overalls all year long, looked all dressed up in a pair of belted pants and long-sleeved white shirt with garters.

Along with the cake, we packed deviled eggs, potato salad and a jar of pickled beets. Finally, Dad backed the Star out of the shed, we scrambled in, stashed the food and, with the warm summer wind in our faces, were off to begin the long-awaited day of fun and games, and special treats.

Several people had already arrived and were busy getting things ready. Dad helped some fellows setting up game booths, one of which was for the baseball throw, which he would run. After we set the food on the long tables in the shade of the big trees, Lester joined the other men, while Dora and I looked for our school friends. We felt a wild abandon at the freedom of the day: no chores, no responsibilities, and a day electrified with the promise of exciting things to come.

By the time the program in the hall was ready to start, most of the setting-up work outside was done. After the Pledge of Allegiance, about twenty men and women of the grange's drill team marched out onto the floor. The women were in white dresses, and the men wore white shirts and pants, brightened by wide blue sashes. With amazing precision, they crisscrossed the hall, going up its length, back and forth across the width. I wondered how they remembered to do everything at just the right time and keep from running into each other. When the drill team finished, we sang *America, the Beautiful,* and the master of the grange introduced the speaker.

The sounds of firecrackers going off, hammering, and the constant drone of men's voices filtered through the open windows, punctuating the speaker's formal address. We couldn't make much sense of what he was saying anyway and wished he'd hurry up and finish. The hall got stuffy, making us fidgety and chomping at the bit to escape. At last the speech was over. The singing of *The Star Spangled Banner* concluded the program, and we all dashed out into the fresh, cool air and the freedom awaiting us outdoors.

The women bustled around arranging food, the grange chaplain said grace, and we got in line clutching our plates. I hardly knew what to take. The tables were loaded with all kinds of food. It was quite a spread. There were salads, casseroles, baked beans, pickles, sandwiches, deviled eggs, pickled beets, red and green Jello, and all kinds of cakes and pies. I kept in mind to save room for a piece of coconut cake, my favorite dessert, so I didn't take a sandwich. I'd gotten my fill of them in school lunches.

After lunch, people tried their skills at the various challenges the booths offered. At one booth, one had to toss a coin into saucers; there was also a ring toss and other games testing one's skills. It was a good thing a lot of people played these games, because part of the proceeds went for prize money in the footraces, and we planned to win our share.

Our favorite booth was the baseball throw. Several times in other years we had won a little celluloid kewpie doll, a set of jacks, a box of Cracker Jacks, and other cherished prizes. Our aims were pretty good after practicing all year by throwing rocks at targets on our long hike to school and back.

Dad worked the baseball throw, which was one of the most popular booths. When a ball hit a doll suspended on an iron pipe, the doll spun like it was doing somersaults. If the ball hit the top part, the doll went over backwards; if it hit the lower part, it spun frontwards. Hitting them wasn't as easy at it looked. A two-inch fringe around each doll made them appear bigger. When the baseball hit the fringe, it went right on past, making a sharp "thwack" as it hit the canvas behind the dolls.

The baseball throw cost a quarter. Ice cream cones, candy bars, and pop were only a nickel apiece. But I didn't even have a single nickel to buy an ice cream cone or an ice-cold grape soda — not until I'd win some prize money.

When it was time for the races. Lester, Dora and I took off our heavy oxfords. We could run faster in our bare feet, and I just knew we could win some prize money. Paul Holter and Dee McKern started the races with the youngest children, and I was happy when Dora won in the eight-year-olds' race. Soon Paul announced, "All girls eleven years old line up for the next race."

Heart pounding in anticipation of winning, I put my bare toes on the starting line scratched in the dirt road. Six girls leaned forward, waiting for Paul's call, "On your mark, get set, go!"

At the word, "Go," I lunged forward, getting a head start on the others. I ran as fast as I could, until my chest touched the binding twine marking the finish line. When I pulled the twine out of the men's hands, I knew I had won first prize.

Clutching the quarter, I could almost taste the ice cream cones that big coins could buy. I watched the next few events, waiting for the sack races and three-legged races to begin. In the three-legged races, one of our legs was tied to one of our partner's, and we had to keep in step as we ran. It wasn't easy, and kids tumbled to the ground, giggling and laughing. By the end of the race, even the losers were having so much fun that they didn't mind not winning any money.

With so many races going on, every kid who entered won something. We three Riley kids won more than our share of prize money. The first-place prize of a quarter made us feel almost giddy, thinking of all the things we could buy with it — and we had won nickels and dimes to boot.

I made a beeline for the baseball throw and won that coveted kewpie doll. After that, I bought a strawberry ice cream cone and a bottle of that delicious ice-cold grape soda. Both treats tasted better than I remembered from the year before. I also bought a roll of red paper ammunition for my old cap gun. I pointed the toy gun at the sky, pulled the trigger, and banged away. Just when I was looking to buy fireworks, I spotted Chinaman Tai.

Although about a foot shorter than most grown-ups, Chinaman Tai was easy to find. I just listened for his shrill voice as he wandered through the crowd pulling his little red wagon, calling, "Fi cackies, fi cents," in his high, sing-songy voice.

Catching up with Chinaman Tai, I tugged at his loose sleeve to get his attention. He stopped his sing-songy calls and turned around, bringing his face close to mine. As I looked straight into his dark eyes, I was startled that we were the same height. I wondered why a full-grown man was so short. Handing him a dime, I said, "I want two packages of small firecrackers, please."

He bent down to get them from his wagon, which also held neatly stacked novelties from China — magic flowers that "bloomed" when dropped in water and tiny fans and umbrellas, among other things. His small hand picked up the thin, red tissue-wrapped firecrackers and held them out to me. I felt his cool hand as I took them and saw a hint of smile touch his face. Putting my dime in his pocket, he turned and continued through the crowd with his wagon, calling, "Fi cackies, fi cents."

Chinaman Tai was the most unusual person at the celebration. He looked different from the rest of the crowd, had a long black pigtail hanging down his back and spoke so strangely.

We had never heard him called anything but "Chinaman Tai" and never saw him except at the grange hall on the Fourth of July. We had heard that he lived near Daisy and panned for gold in the Columbia. He couldn't have found much, because he always looked like he could stand a good meal.

After the races were over, it was apparent that most of the winners had bought firecrackers. People had a hard time hearing each other talk over the loud bangs of firecrackers going off. A few of the big boys managed to make a lot of noise by not separating their firecrackers, and with one fuse lit, one would go off right after the other. A smoky-blue haze hovered over our heads, and the strong smell of black powder filled our noses.

No one wanted the day of fun to end, but almost everyone had cows to milk and evening chores to do. At about four o'clock in the afternoon, the games and the visiting ended. Firecrackers stopped popping; men took down the canvas booths and closed the hinged sides of the refreshment stand. We packed our belongings into the Star and headed home.

As our old car chugged up the hills, we didn't have much to say. Quietly content and tired after all the excitement, we were satisfied with our wonderful day. Under Mom's watchful eyes, Leola and Effie had waded in the creek and played around the tables with other little girls, having fun in their own way. Lester,

Dora and I had won over a dollar each in the races and had bought everything we wanted. Lester had tucked his cap gun into his pocket; I held on to mine, as well as my new kewpie doll with its bright pink feathers, and Dora clutched her cap gun, afraid she would lose it.

Our parents had had a good time. In between shifts at his booth, Dad took time to talk with his friends. Sitting in the shade, taking care of the little girls, Mom had gotten acquainted with newcomer Letha Peters and visited with old friends she hadn't seen in a while. The only sad note for all of us was knowing we'd have to wait a whole year for the next Fourth-of-July celebration to roll around.

Chinaman Tai died soon after that, in 1937. From then on, our Fourth-of-July celebrations were never the same. We missed seeing him; missed hearing him shout, "Fi cackies, fi cents." Buying our firecrackers at the refreshment stand wasn't as much fun as buying them from the small, pig-tailed man.

⟨⧓⟩ ⟨⧓⟩

Later on we learned more about Chinaman Tai. His full name was Wang Fok Tai. Born in 1860 in China, he was fourteen when he came to Stevens County with his brother, Ah Nim, and their Uncle Dock. The newcomers built a shack of a house near Daisy, not far from the Columbia River, and began placer mining for gold. The three men lived together until 1918, when Uncle Dock died. Word got around that the brothers had found and hidden a large amount of gold. On July fourth, 1919, a small group of likkered-up men rode in on horses to rob them. Finding Ah Nim home alone, they beat him demanding to know where he had hidden the gold. But he died without revealing his secret.

When Chinaman Tai (Wang Fok Tai) died, he was buried next to his brother, Ah Nim, and Uncle Dock in the old cemetery across the road from the Rice school.

Ralph Byrd once told me that Chinaman Tai often picked up and ate chickens that had been killed by cars on the highway. One day when Ralph's father asked Tai how he was feeling, he had replied, "No feel good, no feel good. Ate chicken dead too long."

In the summer of 1993, Lester took me to the cemetery to show me Tai's grave. On the small hill overlooking the highway and the Rice store, he led me across the cemetery access road. Bending down, he brushed aside the dry, white cheat grass to expose the three small markers, "Wang Fok Tai." I felt I had found a piece of my childhood. I wished for a package of firecrackers to set off in memory of this small, foreign man who brought happiness into the lives of a bunch of country kids.

24

Wheat Harvest in the Big Bend

In the summer of 1935, Dad went to work the wheat harvest in the Big Bend. Our farm produced only enough money to cover our bare necessities. To earn extra money, Dad looked for work whenever he had time. Sometimes he worked as a logger, but that summer he had heard of a wheat rancher in the Big Bend Country needing extra hands. There were miles and miles of big wheat ranches in the central and southern part of the state, some spread over more than a thousand acres. Because of the more southerly location and the warmer weather, that grain was ready to harvest before ours was.

The wheat ranchers summer-fallowed about half of their land. But since some still had hundreds of acres planted in wheat, they always needed a lot of extra men to work during the harvest. The wheat had to be cut just as soon as it was ready. If a delay occurred after it ripened, the grain scattered on the ground when it was cut and went to waste.

It was a good time for Dad to work away from home. He had finished planting our oats, barley and spring wheat, cut our green hay and put it in the barn. He could spare some time away from the farm. Our first grain to ripen was the winter wheat, and it wouldn't be ready to harvest until late summer.

On the day he left, the five of us clustered around Mom in front of the house watching him drive away in our old Star. At first we waved, calling goodbye, then just stood silent, watching the empty space between us grow wider and wider. The car disappeared into the bend of the road, and as it went around yet another turn, all we could see was its back end dropping out of sight. Then Dad was gone.

He was heading south to the wheat harvest in the Big Bend country (that's where the Columbia River makes a big bend) about 150 miles away, below Ritzville. Going less than fifty miles an hour, it would take him a good part of the day to get to his destination. He expected to be gone for a month, and we quickly felt an emptiness without him; but Mama was there, so we wouldn't be lonesome. And besides, we had plenty of work to keep us busy.

Lester had to do most of the barn chores by himself. Dora and I had our own work, but we liked the adventure of helping him look for the cows in the hundred-acre pasture and herding them to the barn for the evening milking. After locking them in their stanchions, Lester climbed the ladder into the hay mow and threw hay down into the manger. In addition to milking four cows twice a day, he shoveled the manure out of the gutters every morning after letting the cows out to pasture.

Almost four years old, even little Leola had a job. She also wanted to learn to milk the cows. She carried her own milk bucket — a small lard pail with a bail — to the barn. Lester seated her on a milking stool at the cow's flank and told her, "All you have to do is squeeze a teat and milk will squirt out."

After the twosome brought the milk to the house and Lester had run it through the cream separator, Leola bottle-fed a lamb with some of the separated milk. The little lamb's mother had died in late spring, and Dad had brought the baby into the house to show us how cute it was. Since Leola had been the one to give it its first bottle, the lamb followed her around when she went outside.

At feeding time, Mama filled its bottle with warm milk and pulled a large nipple over the top. As soon as Leola had the bottle in her hand, the baby lamb butted its head against her in eagerness to eat. Our little sister had a hard time getting to the edge of the porch to sit down without getting knocked down.

After finishing with the cows, Lester slopped the hogs. He filled their water trough and carried two or three large buckets of slop from the house — carrot, potato, and beet peelings, other vegetable waste, and two or three gallons of skim milk.

Since I was eleven and the oldest girl, Mama expected me to keep an eye on Leola and Effie. Dora and I took the little ones along with us when we carried water from the well, fed the chickens, gathered the eggs from the chicken house, brought wood into the kitchen, or did other outside chores. The little girls helped us find the eggs and carry firewood. Even Effie, not quite two years old, carried a small stick.

On top of getting our chores done, we weeded our big vegetable garden and helped in the house. We swept the floor, peeled potatoes and did the dishes. Two or three times a week we walked the mile to our mailbox to get our mail. Since we liked running around outside, we didn't call that work, and getting the mail gave us an excuse to visit with the Heideggers for a few minutes. During the time Dad was gone, they always asked how we were doing and offered their help.

After what seemed like a long time — more than a month — Dad came home from the harvest. Stepping out of the car with a big grin on his face, he looked at Mom and said, "Sis, I got a whole pocketful of money," and just kept on grinning. (For a few years I thought Sis was Mom's name, as Dad always called her that instead of her real name, which was Audrey.)

He had made good wages and brought it all home. It was plenty to get us through the summer until he sold the grain from our harvest. Still beaming, he handed Mama the mail he had collected from our mailbox. We were all happy to see him, but none more so than Lester and Mom. Big brother was relieved that he wouldn't have to milk four cows all by himself. And our mother, even though she could count on the Heideggers in an emergency, had felt more isolated than ever without a car. It must have worried her a lot. In talking about it later to a friend, she said, "I don't know what we'd have done while Bill was gone if one of us had gotten hurt so far away from a doctor."

Dad told us about the Big Bend wheat country and his job of sewing grain sacks. He didn't complain about the long hours; accustomed to hard work, he was just happy he'd been able to make some extra money.

A sack sewer's job included helping the teamsters care for the horses. Taking care of the machinery and getting grease or oil on his hands would soften them. For wrestling the rough gunnysacks full of wheat, he needed tough, work-hardened hands. His day started with feeding, watering and harnessing the twenty horses by himself. The day ended with unharnessing and currying the horses and giving them hay, grain and water.

Often the ranchers used more than a team of twenty horses to pull each combine across the rolling wheatland. Three or four combines, depending on the size of the farm, followed each other around the fields, cutting wide swaths in the standing grain. Besides pulling the heavy machine, the horses furnished the power to turn the combines' inner workings that threshed the grain.

Dad's job as sack sewer kept him sitting on the combine in the "dog house," sewing the tops of the bulging grain sacks. The straw and chaff blew out an opening along the back, sending straw trails across the newly cut stubble ground. He had to have great endurance, and be quick, nimble and strong to get the job done. It was grueling work.

There was good money in the harvest. The men were paid wages by the day. A day's work was hot and dusty and lasted from daylight to dark. Dad and the teamster riding on the combine were covered with the dust kicked up around them. The big bull wheel of the heavy combine dug into the field, making furrows where it slewed and slipped around the side hills. A dirty roiling dust cloud hung over the combine, working its way around the golden grain-field, which made it hard to breathe, and layered itself on every exposed inch of the working men.

By the time Dad returned home, our grain was almost ready to bind. The winter wheat had turned golden, but when he broke a head off and shelled the grain into his hand, he pronounced it not quite dry enough; it would be another week before he could start to bind.

Compared to what he had been doing on that big wheat ranch, our harvest was a simple job. He only had to harness four horses to pull the binder, which was much lighter than a combine. It would take him less than a week to bind the grain. The binder cut the grain, gathered it bundles — tying a binding twine around each bundle — then kicked it out into a carrying basket on the side. When it was full, Dad tripped a lever, dumping the six bundles on the ground.

Lester, Dora and I did most of the shocking. We picked up the individual bundles and stacked them in shocks of ten to twelve, ready to be picked up by the bundle wagon and hauled to the threshing machine. If we would have had enough money to buy a combine for threshing the grain as it cut it, we wouldn't have had to do any shocking.

When our old secondhand binder broke down, it took longer to get the binding done. Dad had to go to Colville to get a new part, put it on the binder, and continue cutting the grain, hoping to get done before the binder broke down again and before a hard rain came. Rain and wind could knock the grain down, making it impossible for the binder to cut.

Shortly after Dad returned from one of his trips south to the wheat harvest, a man in Colville told him about a rich farm area — way up north in Alaska. The United States Government was sponsoring a homestead program to entice pioneers to settle the Matanuska Valley, where the land's rich soil and long daylight hours made vegetables grow to huge sizes. The man had gone on to say that Alaska is called the Land of the Midnight Sun because in the summer the sun is still shining at midnight.

Dad came home from town all excited and told Mama about it, saying that the government wanted farmers to move to Alaska and would help them get settled. He added, "The cabbages there grow big as washtubs!"

He talked and talked, trying to convince her it would be a good thing for us to do. We could tell he was itching to grow those giant vegetables. As she listened quietly, we watched her face for some sign of what went on in her mind, afraid it might light up to match Dad's enthusiasm. But she never displayed any interest in uprooting the family and moving to an unknown and faraway place. At the same time, she never said anything against it.

After a few days, when we didn't hear any more talk about going to the Matanuska Valley, Lester and I breathed a sigh of relief. We didn't want to move to Alaska and had been afraid Dad would persuade Mama to pack up and go.

We were also glad Dad didn't decide to go by himself looking for work; Alaska seemed an awful long way. Even if he could grow giant cabbages in Alaska, we didn't want to stand in front of the house watching him drive away again.

In late summer, that area in Alaska made headlines when Will Rogers and his pilot, Wiley Post, were killed in a plane crash on August 15, 1935. Just the day before, Will Rogers had talked to a crowd of settlers in Matanuska for over an hour. Before they took off the next day on what was to be their last flight, he sent his daily news dispatch talking about the seven or eight hundred settlers in the Matanuska Valley

⊰≋° ⊰≋°

Forty years later while vacationing in the Matanuska Valley, I saw several of those homesteads, now abandoned. I realized how wise Mom had been in her desire to stay put on our farm in Washington instead of going on a wild goose chase to Alaska.

25

Three New Additions

In the fall of 1935, Dad traded in our old Star as part payment on a secondhand Nash sedan. This was the first major change since Effie was born almost three years ago. The Star had been our means of transportation for eight years, and I always thought we would keep it forever. It had brought us from Oregon, a long distance away, and had taken us over many miles of road since then.

But soon I wasn't missing the old car at all. The Nash offered much better protection from the weather, with its metal top and real glass windows that cranked up and down. No longer could the wind blow in like it had through the gaps of the Star's isinglass side curtains. The best thing about the new car was the automatic starter button on the floor of car. All you had to do was step on it with your foot and the engine would start. The only times Dad had to crank it was on cold mornings and the few times when the battery had run down.

It was a good thing we got a better car. Mama no longer worried so much about keeping the babies warm. In the coldest part of the winter, on January 19, 1936, she gave birth to twin girls and named them Viola and Vida.

On that day, soon after Lester, Dora and I had ridden off to school on the horses, Mama's labor pains had started. For the third time, she would go to Mrs. Aldredge's Maternity Home in Kettle Falls. Dad dropped off Leola and Effie at the Heideggers' on their way. When we returned home from school, we knew before getting into the house that Mama's time must have come — there was no smoke curling up out of the chimney. Kicking the horses into a trot, we rode to the barn, tied them into the stalls, and ran to the house. It was just like we figured. Mama had left a note.

The house was cold without a fire and was so empty without the rest of our family. In less than ten minutes we had a good fire going in living room and kitchen stoves. Lester went out to milk the cows and do the other evening chores, while I started supper and lit the kerosene lamp. I prepared a simple meal from leftovers, cooked potatoes and made gravy just like Mama taught me. When Lester came back from doing the chores, we ate our supper. Dora and I had just finished doing the dishes when the Nash went by the house to park in the shed.

It was no surprise that Mama was having another baby. Even before she told us, we had figured it out because she started to get big. But when Dad came in with Leola and Effie in tow and announced that our mother had given birth to twin girls, that was a surprise.

Because of the icy, snow-covered roads, we didn't get to see her while she was at Mrs. Aldredge's house. We missed her and were glad at the end of ten days to get back from school and find her at home and meet our twin sisters.

The first week Mom was home, she wrote a letter to the Montgomery Ward Company in Portland, Oregon. She had ordered a layette for the new baby the previous November and had noticed that the company would furnish a second layette free of charge to anyone having twins. What a blessing! Mama notified them of the happy event.

A couple of weeks later, there was a bulky package from Montgomery Ward in our mailbox. The second layette had arrived with the same number of nightgowns, kimonos, shirts, receiving blankets, safety pins, and Birds Eye diapers as the first one. We had enough clothes for both girls, and they hadn't cost anything.

With the two new babies, there were nine people in our family, which meant a lot of work for everyone. We had to do a great deal more laundry, scrubbing diapers and other baby clothes on the washboard, and carrying extra buckets of water from the well. In the bitter cold, the clothes froze soon after we hung them on the line and were stiff as boards when we carried them in the house. There were always diapers and baby clothes either on the line or waiting to be folded, and the water buckets were always empty.

When Mama didn't have enough milk to feed two babies, she put them on the bottle. We made do with empty medicine bottles fitted with rubber nipples, instead of having to buy baby bottles in the store. The flat shape of the medicine bottles made them easy to hold without slipping out of our hands. Dora and I had almost a full-time job caring for the babies, from feeding and bathing to changing their diapers.

Despite the work they caused, the twins were good and lovable babies; they didn't fuss or cry except when they were hungry or wet.

The severe cold kept us indoors, and caring for the twins — despite the work — gave us something to do. One change brought on others: we had twin sisters, a new car, and in February we moved to another farm with a house that had water piped to it from a creek. That was just the beginning of change.

Part IV
1936 – 1944

Home Place

26

Moving to Home Place

In the fall of 1935, Sam Curry drove up to our house in his shiny black car. After the greetings were over, he got down to the real purpose of his visit and told Dad that he and Effie were going to move to Asotin, Washington and would be selling the farm. He said, "Why don't you and Audrey buy it so you won't have to pay rent anymore?"

Dad replied, "You're asking a fair price, Sam, but I don't have that much cash. I'm afraid to borrow from the bank because I've seen too many people lose their farms when they couldn't make the payments."

Sam and Effie sold their farm, and Dad went looking for a place to rent with enough acreage to make a living. He had heard the old Root Place on the other side of Rupert's land was for rent. It was sandwiched between the two roads leading up to Rickey

Canyon. The house was at the southern edge of the property, less than a mile north of our school.

The house was small, and only about half of the 140 acres could be farmed. The rest of the land was either timbered or too hilly to plow. A spring fed into a small creek running through the lower portion of the farm and supplied the house with water. Another spring was on the far side, where the cattle could water when grazing in that area.

A barbed-wire fence about a quarter of a mile above the house separated the cultivated land from the pasture and kept the livestock out of the grainfields. Connecting the two parts was a wagon road which started below the barn and chicken house, crossed the creek and wound up the steep hill behind the barn, then led on to the fields. (That road was so steep that a few years later Dad had a new road bulldozed out of a more gradual slope, which made the downhill trip in a hay wagon less dangerous.)

Dad wondered how he could fit nine people into a one-bedroom house. Fortunately, the house had a large attic which could be made into a dormitory bedroom for us kids. Since the farm was available and we needed a place to live, Dad decided to rent it despite the lack of space.

When he told the Heideggers that we would be moving, Abe said sadly, "Bill, we hate to see you leave. You and Audrey have been good neighbors."

In isolated areas where neighbors relied on each other for help, a good neighbor could mean the difference between life and death. When Abe said our parents had been good neighbors, it was the highest compliment he could give. The Heideggers had been good neighbors to us as well.

Moving day came in late February of 1936. Dora and I had to walk to school that day, using shanks' ponies instead of riding Betty because she was needed to pull the wagon. Lester stayed home from school and would help make the several trips hauling our belongings to the new place. Although there was a few inches of snow left, Dad hoped the team he drove could pull the iron-wheeled wagon without mishap if he kept his loads light. Lester drove a team of two horses pulling the big bobsled with its double set of iron-plated wooden runners. Using the wagon and the bobsled would make for less trips.

After school, Dora and I felt strange to be heading home in the "wrong" direction. We wouldn't have to walk those three long miles anymore; our new place was less than a mile away, and all by road. "Come on, Dora, let's see how long it will take us to get home today," I said. "I'll bet we can get there in less than half an hour."

Twenty minutes later, we arrived at our new home and found Mama there with the four little girls. It had taken several trips to bring our things from the old place and get the kitchen stove working to warm up the house.

Dad still had to make the attic into a large bedroom, which presented a few problems. There was no heat, no stairway and no closet. There was no covering over the rafters. They were bare and we could see daylight shining through a few gaps in the shingles. It would be cold in winter without heat, except for the little warmth that would get through the floor from downstairs, and there would be some heat from the brick chimney.

The boards on the overhang above the front porch had to be removed in order to get upstairs. The attic part overhanging the porch made the upstairs space bigger than the downstairs.

After climbing a ladder Dad had propped against the end of the house, he used his claw hammer to pull the nails out of several of the wide boards which were nailed horizontally across the end. He carefully lowered them to Lester, who stacked them because Dad would nail them back up when our beds had been moved upstairs.

Lester tied a rope on a bedstead and Dad hoisted it up, until two dressers, three link springs, bedsteads, and mattresses had made it up. When that was done, the two of them made a trapdoor and a ladder leading up the outside of the house under the porch overhang. It would be our only access after the boards were nailed back on the end of the house.

Dad sawed out a square space in the attic floor directly above the outside wall of the house near the front door, made a trapdoor with two leather hinges — and we were ready to move into our new bedroom-dormitory.

To serve as the ladder, he nailed two two-by-four boards to the wall vertically and added crosspieces for rungs. That's how we got upstairs to our attic bunkroom. The twins would sleep in their oversized crib in our parents' bedroom. Everyone had a place to sleep, and Dad proved he could fit all nine of us into a one-bedroom house.

A fire was going in both stoves, and Mom was busy putting dishes and pots and pans in the cupboards when Dora and I arrived from school. Since Mom was there, it didn't feel unfamiliar, just different. She immediately put us to work peeling potatoes for supper.

Soon Dad and Lester were coming down the hill by the barn, herding the cows ahead of the loaded bobsled, which was piled high with farm equipment, hay and the grain box. Dora and I rushed to the barn, where the men were unloading the big wooden grain box. With a lot of effort, they carried the cumbersome load through the door into the cow barn. After getting the grain box in place, Dad said, "That was a heavy sonofabitch. I'm glad we don't have to move every day."

At about five feet ten, Dad was sturdy and solidly built. He was brawny and muscular from all his hard physical labors. He probably weighed about 180 pounds, none of which was fat.

⋘ ⋙

Alvin Conner, a school friend, recently told me that he had been impressed by Dad's brute strength. Apparently when helping the Conner family move, he had carried a heavy cast-iron kitchen stove all by himself for some distance.

⋘ ⋙

A few days later Dad and Lester took the bobsled to move the last of the hay and grain into our new barn. We watched as they tossed it into the hay mow with their pitchforks, and carried sacks of oats to dump into the grain box. They took the rest of the of grain sacks to the "granary," which was the old house that had been left standing when the "new" house was built about twenty-five years earlier. It was an ugly, two-story, yellowish building about twenty feet from our house. To separate the different kinds of grain, Dad had built grain bins in two of the big downstairs rooms, into which he emptied the last of the sacks of wheat, rye, barley and oats. In the next few days he and Lester brought the rest of the farm equipment to our new farm.

Moving day hadn't been the first time Lester and I had seen our new house. We had been there a few years earlier when our teacher, Arlean Dean, had lived there. She had invited all her pupils for some special occasion. We had no way of knowing that some day we'd be shocking grain in those fields and living in her house. Miss Dean had served the first red Kool-Aid we'd ever had and we were so impressed with its flavor that we had to tell Mom about it before telling her anything else about the party.

Going to bed that first night was really different. It felt strange to have to open the front door and go outside in the cold. It didn't take the five of us long to scamper up the ladder to the attic and close the trapdoor behind us. I tucked the covers around Leola and

Effie in their bed, then crawled in beside Dora. Lester had a double bed all to himself on the other side of the chimney.

After living in our new house for a week and making the short walk to school, we realized how much easier it was compared to what we'd been doing for the past five years. Despite all the adventures we had enjoyed on the Curry Place, we had gotten awfully tired of making the almost-six-mile-round trip to school on foot — especially going home, which was uphill most of the way.

We knew without being told that we wouldn't be riding the horses the short distance to school. But we could still ride around, exploring our new farm and the surrounding land at the foot of Monumental Mountain in the Huckleberry Mountain Range.

⊰❧ ❧⊱

A few years later Dad and Mom bought this farm. After we kids left home, they had the money to have the house remodeled — they put in an indoor bath, an automatic washer and dryer and an inside stairway to the attic. Mom finally had an easier life. This farm would be their "home place" for the rest of their lives.

27

Our New Home

After living a few days in our new home, we felt we belonged. Even the bedtime adventure of going out the front door to go upstairs became routine. The first one to arrive lit the small kerosene lamp. The last one up the ladder closed the trapdoor and pulled a small rug over it to prevent the wind from blowing in. A pole between rafters with a few nails sticking up held our dresses, overalls and shirts. We shared a small dresser on our side, and Lester had one all to himself on his part of the attic. We didn't have many clothes and didn't miss the convenience of having a closet.

Since there were no boards to cover the rafters, heat escaped through the roof in winter, and we could see the shingles in daylight. Heat rose up from downstairs through the rough floorboards, and the brick chimney gave off some warmth. Dora and I had a big, cozy bearskin beside our bed, and on cold mornings we ran our bare feet across the thick fur for instant warmth.

While Mom was cooking supper, Dora and I put two flatirons on the stove to heat. By bedtime the irons were hot, and we wrapped each one in layers of cloth and put them under the covers at the foot of our beds. The next morning, we returned the cold irons to the kitchen so they'd be handy for that night's bedwarming.

Each bed had several warm quilts that Mom had made. The tops were colored cotton scraps sewn together in a crazy-quilt pattern, with cotton batting inside and outing flannel for the bottom. They were lighter weight and prettier than the drab wool coverlets she had made from a mine's discarded sacks. The sack material was coarse and heavy, neither pretty nor pleasant to the touch, and Mom regretted having spent the time and work on making the no-cost coverlets.

Every fall before cold weather set in, our parents went to J.C. Penney's in Colville and bought enough flannel sheets for all the beds. The sheets came in pink and white or blue and white with wide stripes, and were long enough to serve as both top and bottom and lasted the winter.

At night, Dad kept only a low fire going in the heating stove, getting up once or twice to add another chunk of wood. The cookstove's firebox was too small to hold an all-night wood supply, so we let its fire go out. First one up in the morning, Dad added more wood to the embers in the heating stove and started a fire in the cookstove. In spite of all the effort, the house was still cold when the rest of us got up. On the coldest mornings, when we couldn't stand the thought of getting dressed in the cold attic, we grabbed our clothes and hurried down the ladder and into the house to dress in the warmth of the roaring heating stove. After nights with below-zero temperatures, ice had formed on the edges of the kitchen sink, and in order to keep the pipe from freezing, we let a good trickle of water run all night. During hot summer days, cooling off the attic was a lot easier than keeping it warm. We just opened the window in each end of the attic, left the trapdoor open, and the cool night air from the mountain rushed in, getting rid of the day's stored-up heat.

Open windows occasionally invited unwelcome company. One night a bat zipped over our heads in the darkness. Afraid it would get tangled in our hair, we ducked under the covers. Finally, Lester waved his arm around wildly and the bat flew out. Before we had learned that bats ate bugs and insects, we had killed the invader. Examining the little furry gray creature and finding how soft and silky it felt, we regretted our deed. With big ears and fur-like skin, the little thing looked more like a friendly mouse than a bird, in spite of its odd-looking transparent wings.

⬧ ⬧

The outside ladder to the attic is gone. A few years after I graduated from high school and left home, Dad and a neighbor, Roy Lickfold, built inside stairs, which was, of course, a lot more convenient.

⬧ ⬧

The best feature about our new place was the short walk to and from school. We didn't have to leave home as early in the morning to get to class on time. And since it was downhill all the way, we could make the distance in twenty minutes. We could even walk to school separately, which we were not allowed to do before. But traveling as a threesome had become such a habit that we left the house together and stayed together. Snow still covered most of the ground, but in Adkins' open field below our house, a few black patches of dirt showed through where the snow had melted.

Low brush crowded both sides of the gravel road as it dropped downhill and bent to the left. Although Quillisascut Creek ran alongside, we could catch only glimpses of it through its dense screen of tamarack, cedar and fir trees.

I was almost twelve and old enough to be glad that Leola, who would start school that fall, would never have to make the long walk from the Curry Place to get to class. Our new home, situated on a well-traveled road, made the school just a hop and a skip away.

Soon the strangeness of being in a different house wore off. Dad's farm work didn't change much, but Mom's life became easier. Having cold water piped into the kitchen seemed like quite a luxury, and she enjoyed it. A pipe stuck into the creek brought water right to the kitchen sink, and she would never have to face an empty water bucket. The sink alone was a big help because a drainpipe took the waste water to an open ditch. We still had to heat water on the cookstove, but even that seemed easier.

The only drawback was getting to our room upstairs. In the beginning, bedtime was an adventure, but when February's icy winds gusted, chilling us to the bone before we scrambled through the trapdoor, we no longer considered the climb fun.

There was another ladder in the house that led to the cellar under the house from a trapdoor between the dining and living rooms, where two big wooden bins stored potatoes, carrots, and big Hubbard squash, and jars of canned vegetables and fruit lined several shelves. Having the cellar under the house instead of outdoors was especially convenient during the cold winter days.

Water in the kitchen was sort of a miracle, and equal to that of Dad's purchasing a gasoline-powered washing machine with some money he had managed to scrape up. "It's something like starting that old Harley Davidson motorcycle I used to have. You have to step down on this pedal as hard as you can," he explained the workings of the new washer to us.

As soon as the motor was running, the deafening racket from the washing machine sounded just like the roar of a motorcycle. When the machine ran out of gas, the unexpected silence startled us, filling the space where the throbbing and pounding had been until we replenished the gas and restarted the motor.

The wringer attached to the washer could swing around into different positions, and we ran the clean clothes from the washer through the wringer rollers into the first rinse tub, then pressed a lever and swung the wringer around into position between the two rinse tubs. It was easier and faster than wringing the clothes out by hand or putting them through the hand-cranked wringer. Our new washer saved us many hours of backbreaking work of scrubbing clothes on the washboard.

One day I was careless and let a fold catch my hand and carry it through the wringer. Mom had shown us how to use the pressure-release lever, but all I could do was yell for her. She was beside me me in two steps, hitting the lever on top of the wringer, and I pulled my hand free. Luckily, I wasn't hurt.

A floor-to-ceiling cupboard between the kitchen and dining room with access from both sides gave us good storage space. The linoleum-covered work cabinet with its big bins stood near the sink, and patterned linoleum covered most of the floor. The cookstove was the most important — and the biggest — object in the kitchen, had an unending need for wood, and kept us busy just filling the woodbox. The stove's metal back held a double warming oven, which projected partway over the cooking surface. A water reservoir, attached to one side of the stove level with the top, held two buckets of water, which heated when a fire was going.

We still used the cream separator, which had been bolted to the floor in the kitchen. It was an important item in our kitchen — twice a day we separated the cream from the whole milk. After attaching a cloth to the metal separator bowl with clothespins, we poured the milk through to strain out dirt that might have fallen into the buckets. Although Dora and I were able to turn the handle, Lester was usually the one who did the job.

Washing the separator parts took longer and was a more disagreeable job. At night, we just ran warm water through to rinse its disks and other parts, but in the morning, Mom took the separator apart to wash the pieces in hot, soapy water.

The cabinet provided the only work surface in the kitchen. It had three shallow drawers at the top and two big pull-out bins below. The right-hand bin held six or seven loaves of home-made bread; the one on the left held half of a fifty-pound sack of flour. When I turned twelve, Mom expected me to keep the flour bin filled.

Lester was older and stronger and could carry a fifty-pound sack of flour easily. But when he wasn't around, it was up to me to lug a sack to the kitchen from an upstairs room of the "old" house next door, where Dad had built a large platform, suspending it from the ceiling with wires to keep mice from getting at the sacks of flour.

It was all I could do to wrestle a sack off the platform onto my shoulder and keep it balanced while going down the stairs, crossing the yard, and climbing the steps to our porch. After easing it to the floor beside the cabinet, I untied the two interwoven strings at the top, hoisted the sack up again, and poured half the flour into the bin.

The dining room held a rough table, two chairs, two benches, and a tall oak dish cabinet. We sat on benches on either side of the table, and our parents occupied the chairs at the end near the kitchen. The living room furniture consisted of a black leather reclining couch, a rocking chair, Mom's New Home treadle sewing machine, a straight chair and the big heating stove. The bedroom was barely big enough for Mom and Dad's bed, the twins' large crib, and a dresser. The place was small, but it was home.

Frank Rupert's Landslide

"Bill, I want you to bring all my land back and put it up on the hillside where it belongs," Frank Rupert kidded as he stood looking at the landslide.

Dad stared in disbelief at the five-foot-high pile of earth covering part of our field. The mass had slid off Frank's hill, carrying trees, bushes and part of the barbed-wire fence with it, crossed the county road, and oozed onto our land. Shocked to see part of his level field turned into an unusable brushy mound, Dad replied, "By grab, Frank, I'd sure like to; I won't be able to plant any oats there with all those trees!"

Both men knew nothing could be done about the dirt and the trees, so they might as well joke about it. The winter snows had been deep, and heavy spring rains had added even more moisture to the ground, which made the earth ooze like hot fudge. The rain stopped and both men had gone out to check for damage, with Lester and me tagging along. Frank Rupert was there when we arrived, standing beside the landslide piled on the road which separated the two farms.

Frank's head turned as he looked up at the yawning gash on his brushy hillside, then down to the huge pile of dirt blocking the road and extending into our grainfield, which had broken and carried with it a section of barbed-wire fence and buried another portion. The bushes and small quaking aspens that had been rooted to the hillside slid right along with the dirt, coming to rest right side up, as if they'd been growing in our field for years.

Eventually, the county road crew arrived with a bulldozer and scraper to remove the dirt and clear the road, which was part of the rural mail route and had to be opened quickly. But they couldn't use county equipment to remove the landslide from our field. Since neither Dad nor Frank had a bulldozer, the pile stayed where it had come to rest.

Frank didn't care that some of his hillside was gone, but the unwanted pile of dirt stole part of our farmland and was a nuisance, to say the least. Dad would have to go around it every time he plowed, harrowed, mowed, raked or used the binder.

I felt sorry for him that a piece of easy-to-work ground was taken out of use. Much of our land was on sidehills, where he had to be careful so the machinery wouldn't tip over. That spot, now useless, would have yielded twenty or thirty bundles of oats. Dad didn't hold Frank to blame for his loss of working ground — it was just one of the things that go wrong on a farm. The two men appreciated each other as friends and neighbors and were always willing to help. Frank didn't have a good water supply, so Dad let him pipe into a spring on our farm not far from the landslide and let him use the water for free as long as he lived there.

The landslide gave Frank an opportunity to get even with my father for the joke he'd played on him a few years ago. Remembering the coyote "steaks" Dad had sent him, Frank now felt he had something to kid him about. For years afterwards, their usual greeting to each other was, "Hey, Frank, how were those coyote steaks I sent over to you?"

Frank's response was always, "I'll let you know, Bill, when you bring my hillside back to me!"

29

A Birthday Cake

Looking for brown sugar to make a birthday cake, I rummaged through the kitchen cupboard. I moved all the packages and boxes, searched every shelf, went through the cabinet's pull-out bins holding the sugar and flour, and even peered under the sink without finding any.

It was May 27, 1936, Dora's ninth birthday. Mom often hid the brown sugar because one of us was apt to eat it when we got a craving for sweets. No matter how much she baked, desserts didn't last long.

Instead of cakes or cinnamon rolls for dessert, we usually had canned peaches, prunes, apricots or cherries. Of all the fruit, I liked peaches best. They were sweet, having been dead ripe when we picked and canned them. Canned prunes were good, too. We poured cream over them in our bowls and made swirly patterns with our spoons, blending the white cream with the purple juice. Seeing the pretty swirls, Dora had once exclaimed, "I want a dress just like that!"

Dora and I decided to make a spice cake for her birthday because the Raleigh man had been around, and Mom had stocked up on spices. All we needed was brown sugar, and I asked Mom where it was. Without saying a word, she got up from the sewing machine, went to the kitchen cupboard and, standing on tiptoes, reached up to the top shelf and fished around behind some sacks. She brought out her hidden box of brown sugar and said, "Here it is. If it had been a snake, it would have bitten you!"

Mom made this statement to me on many occasions. Everyone in the family knew I had trouble finding things — even if they were staring me right in the face.

Mom had taught us how to lay a fire that would start easily and get going fast. With the damper on the stovepipe as well as the draft open, the fire would draw. Opening the drop-down door in the firebox at the front of the stove, I lit the paper with a match from the tin box on the wall behind the stove and closed the door.

Letting the fire roar for a couple of minutes, I closed the damper in the stovepipe a little. After about five minutes, I added another piece of wood and again adjusted the damper, this time turning it until it was straight across the stovepipe. We'd have too hot a fire if we left both the damper and the draft wide open. From now until our cake was baked, we would control the heat by making adjustments only with the draft and by the amount of wood we fed the stove.

Dora and I started the cake. The big green mixing bowl was almost too heavy and awkward to handle, but it was the right size. I measured the lard and sugar into it, then mixed them together; Dora sifted flour, salt baking powder and spices together.

Leaving her to add the eggs and other ingredients and mix them into the lard and sugar, I went to tend the fire, which needed more wood. I was glad we had bought a newer cookstove; the old one didn't have a temperature gauge, and we had to guess how hot the oven was by how long the fire had been burning.

When Dora had stirred the ingredients together, I took over and beat the batter until my arm got tired. I poured the batter into two round cake pans and placed them into the oven, one at a time. The gauge indicated the heat was just right, but we had to keep a steady fire going until the cakes were done.

We made frosting which didn't look too difficult and was perfect for a spice cake. I used the point of a paring knife to draw a big number NINE in the soft butterscotch frosting. When we licked the pan, we decided we had picked out the best frosting in the whole cookbook.

After supper that night, everyone ate birthday cake for dessert instead of canned fruit. In his usual joking manner, Dad gave it his highest praise: "That's almost fit to eat!"

30

Sewing Lessons

Mom sat at her New Home sewing machine making a cotton housedress for herself. Pushing the treadle made the wheels and gears turn, and forced the needle to go up and down. She held the flowered material firmly with both hands to ensure a straight seam, and guided it under the presser foot.

She made sewing look like magic when she turned a flat piece of material into something to wear. But to her, it was simple, and she didn't consider sewing new clothes "work" — it was more enjoyable than the never-ending job of patching and mending. Leftover pieces of fabric were turned into squares for her "crazy" quilts. Instead of using a quilt pattern, she sewed scraps of all shapes and sizes together, until the piece was large enough to make a quilt.

Watching her made me want to learn how to sew and had my first lesson. First Mom taught me how to sew straight, by giving me two long scraps of material, instructing me to stitch them together as straight I could. I put the two edges together, lowered the presser foot on them, and pushed the treadle with my right foot. When I finished, I cut the threads and looked at the seam. I practiced sewing strips together until my stitching was almost straight.

Mom looked at my strips and said, "It looks like you're ready to sew some quilt pieces together. But first you'll have to cut them out."

She cut out a triangular pattern from a piece of cardboard and showed me how to hold the cardboard pattern onto the material and trace around it with a pencil. Then she instructed me to cut four pieces of each color for each quilt block. Alternating colors created a quilt block that looked like a paper pinwheel spinning in the wind. In the beginning I had some trouble keeping my seams even and making the pieces the same size. I had to rip and start all over again.

Besides piecing together quilt tops, patching overalls, and making dresses and blouses, Mom also used flour sacks to make her brassieres and the cotton bloomers for the four little girls.

In my spare time, I continued making quilt blocks until I had a stack of them. But in my eagerness to see the finished block, I was careless with the seams, so I ended up with different-sized blocks. Although I never got my quilt put together, I *did* learn how to sew a straight seam with a treadle sewing machine.

⟨⟩ ⟨⟩

These early lessons helped me in later years, when I made clothes for myself and my children. But despite Mom's patient training and all my experience, I still have to rip out seams and start over. And, just like Mom, I've learned that patching overalls isn't nearly as much fun as making new clothes.

The Other Side of the Mountain

Propped up on our elbows, Lester, Dora and I sprawled out on the linoleum floor of the livingroom. We were reading a month's accumulation of Sunday funnies that Clarence and Oma Chinn had given us. We liked all the comics but were especially anxious to see what Maggie and Jiggs and the Katzenjammer Kids were doing. After scanning them quickly, we read them again slowly — not missing a word. Mom read aloud to Effie and Leola, who sat close enough to see the pictures.

About twice a month, when we had finished our day's chores and special jobs, we headed out to visit the neighbor kids. Lester liked to play with Don and Howard Borland, the closest neighbors to the north, and that's were we went first. It was a steady climb for half a mile through tall fir and cedar trees that shaded the road. Dora and I trudged along beside Lester until he turned in on the road leading to the Borlands. We kept going a mile farther to visit Bonnie and Sonny (Clarence) Chinn.

From where we stood, we could see almost all of our grain-fields and pasture. Rupert's rangeland was due west, and Heide's farm was to the north. To our right, Monumental Mountain rose up, a wall of evergreens above Borland's grain field. Spread out behind us were the Holter and Loven farms, beyond which the straight line of the Pleasant Valley Road climbed Folsom Hill. Ahead of us, our road ran alongside the barbed-wire fence bordering Borland's land.

A year younger than I, Sonny was the only kid I knew who took music lessons, and I wondered if he would play his violin for us. But the squawks coming out of his violin didn't sound like music — they sounded more like cats fighting.

When we had ridden our horses to school, we often arrived at the barn the same time the Chinn kids got there on their mounts, which gave us something in common. Their parents almost always gave us a fat roll of comics saved from the *Spokesman-Review*'s Sunday paper, which came by mail, and not many people subscribed to it. After supper, we untied the string, let the colorful pages spill out across the floor and caught up on our favorite comics.

I especially liked visiting my classmate, Arlene Conner, whose family lived up the narrow Day Road east of the school-house. She was a lot of fun and always found something to laugh about. Her brother, Alvin, who inherited a slide rule, said he hoped to be an engineer someday. Arlene and I enjoyed talking together while Alvin worked arithmetic problems and their mother played solitaire on the kitchen table.

Most of the visits to our neighbors never lasted long. We just enjoyed going somewhere to see our friends for a while, looking for adventure on the way, watching for deer and getting a look at the other side of the mountain. By the end of summer, we three older kids had traipsed all over the countryside and visited just about all our friends who lived within a three-mile radius.

32

Visiting at Ella Loven's

It was the summer of 1937. I was thirteen years old and was staying with the elderly Mary Carter while her daughter, Ella Loven, and her granddaughter, Barbara, went to Spokane on an overnight shopping trip. Ella didn't want her mother to be left alone that long and had asked me to stay with her. They lived in a white house, about a hundred yards off the road, on hilly land that fanned out below Carter Canyon.

I swung open a small gate and took the shortcut through Ella's alfalfa field that led to her yard. A mountain stream kept the grass green and watered the profusion of candy-colored flowers around her house. The tree-shaded house and lawn reminded me of the oasis pictured in my schoolbook and made the nearby cheat-grass hills look hot and dry.

Everything about the house impressed me, especially the Chinese coins, which were hanging by their braided cord on the wall behind the heating stove. Red cord strung through the square holes in the coins' centers laced them together in the shape of a sword. The coins made me think of Chinaman Tai, who sent to China for the firecrackers he sold at our Fourth-of-July celebrations.

After Ella left, Mrs. Carter handed me a basket and asked me to gather eggs from the henhouse. I had rummaged through the straw-filled nests, found enough eggs to fill the basket, and headed back. Suddenly, a big rooster came flying around the corner of the shed, and with a flurry of wings, it jumped up on me, raking me with its sharp talons. If it hadn't been for my sturdy denim overalls, he would have bloodied my legs.

I didn't dare run for fear of breaking the eggs. Being near the fence at the edge of the barnyard, I scampered up on a post to escape the feisty rooster. I thought he'd leave and take off after some new interest. But he didn't. He just kept strutting around my perch, peering up balefully, and occasionally flying up to get at me. Standing guard below, he had me treed on the fencepost.

I was trapped atop my narrow perch, holding the basket full of eggs. To steady me on my precarious position, I had hooked the heels of my oxfords over a lower strand of the barbed-wire fence separating the barnyard from the house. Finally, I heard a door squeak and saw Mrs. Carter, white hair piled atop her head, hobbling along. She said, "I forgot to warn you about that mean old rooster," and with that, whacked him over the head with her cane.

Relieved, I climbed down, with every egg intact. Until my meeting with Ella's rooster, I had been sure I could tackle almost anything. Before I was ten, I had battled with yellow jackets by knocking down their nests, and fearlessly helped kill deadly rattlesnakes. To let a mere rooster buffalo me was embarrassing.

The next day I again gathered eggs and this time buffaloed the rooster by shaking a stick at him. After throwing some grain out for the chickens, I filled the woodbox and helped Mrs. Carter cook, wash dishes and sweep the floor.

Ella's cookie jar was full of peanut butter cookies, and I was invited to help myself. I remembered my manners and managed to leave a few cookies, which was hard to do; they were sure good!

I was ready to go home. I hadn't found anything interesting to read, and there was no one to play with, but I couldn't leave until Ella and Barbara returned from their shopping trip. I wonder how Barbara felt not having any brothers or sisters. All at once I realized I was lonesome for my family. My parents weren't telling me what to do, and Lester and my sisters weren't here to argue or play with. We were a rowdy bunch of kids, always doing things together, and I missed the hubbub, the action and laughter of our house. It was lovely here, but too quiet and uneventful for my tomboy ways.

Ella and Barbara returned, loaded down with packages, and upended their paper sacks onto the table. Bright colors like the flowers of her garden came spilling out, turning into pieces of cotton dress material. Ella had said she would bring back material for a new dress for me. She spread the pieces out with the sweep of her hand and said, "You can take your pick — pick out the one you like best."

They were all pretty. There were blue, lavender, pink and green pieces with pretty little flowers all over. But the one my eyes locked on had bold stripes of brown and yellow. It looked dashing — that was my choice. Before I headed for home, clutching my new material in its brown paper sack, Ella said, "Now remember, Ines, if your mother doesn't have time to sew up that dress, come back and I'll make it for you."

Her offer surprised me. She had to do most of her own farming, because her husband had died some time ago. Although Barbara was her only child, she probably didn't have as much spare time as Mom, who had seven children. Like others in Pleasant Valley, Ella farmed with horses. Feeding, harnessing and hitching horses to farm machinery was quite a job before she ever started in on the farm work. When Ella worked outside, she wore bib overalls, but as soon as she finished her farm work, she cleaned up and changed into a dress.

It didn't take me long to walk home — it was downhill most of the way. Mom no sooner admired my new dress fabric than she put me to work peeling potatoes. I was happy to be back in the bustle of our home life again. The long hours with no one to play with had shown me how much my large family meant to me.

A week later Mom said, "I have a lot of things to do, so it might be quite a while before I can get around to making your dress. Go over and ask Ella if she still has time to make it."

So back I went, carrying my material. Ella was in the house and didn't seem surprised to see me. When I asked her if she would have time to make my dress, she quickly replied, "Yes. In fact, I have a little spare time right now."

She showed me her dress patterns and said, "Maybe you can find something you like. We're about the same height, but you're thinner than I am, so I'll have to alter the pattern."

I picked a princess dress without a belt. It was double-breasted, had four buttons in two rows, and was the first pattern in that style I'd ever seen. I thought the yellow-and-brown-striped material would look good with the stripes running up and down. After Ella took my measurements, she told me to come back in a few days to see how it fit.

When I went back the following week, she had the dress put together for a fitting and I eagerly pulled the dress on over my head, expecting to look dashing, just like the material. But the dress just hung on me, looking baggy at the waist. Gathering up the looseness with both hands, Ella said she could easily take in the fullness.

Barbara and I went outside to play, and by the time we went back into the house, Ella had the dress finished except for the hem. I tried it on again. It fit perfectly, and I thought perhaps it did make me look a bit dashing. I had a new dress to wear when I entered eighth grade the coming fall. The dress was doubly special because Ella had made it for me — and because it was so bright and bold, it would make me happy to wear it.

Earlier in the summer, Barbara had invited me to stay so she could have someone to play with. Mom told me I could go, but to mind my manners and return right after breakfast. This longer visit gave us a chance to talk about a lot of things, including what we wanted to buy when we grew up. In addition to a swimming pool, Barbara wanted a car in a quiet color, perhaps dark blue. Admiring her taste and wanting to be like her, I said, "I want a quiet color for my car, too, only it's going to be a pale yellow convertible."

When she laughed at my remark, I realized that yellow wasn't exactly a "quiet" color, and I had to laugh, too.

We took turns on the swing tied to a high limb of a maple tree and had long, swooping rides. Barefooted, we watered the lawn, enjoying the water squashing up through our toes as we moved the sprinkler from place to place.

My visit with Barbara introduced me to the pleasures and convenience of indoor plumbing, and I had my first bath in a real tub. Ella had one of the few inside bathrooms in the valley, complete with a tub long enough to stretch my legs. It was a lot roomier than our round galvanized metal washtub, in which I had to draw my knees up almost to my chin. My long legs made up most of my five-foot, six-inch-height.

Taking a bath at Ella's was so easy. The hot-water tank behind the cookstove heated water whenever a fire was going. All I had to do to fill the tub was turn on the faucets and out poured hot and cold water. When I was finished, I just pulled the plug and the water ran out by itself. I didn't have to lug the tub to the door and pour the water out like we did at home. The only thing left to do was to scrub out the tub with cleanser. I knew that if our house had a real bathtub, I'd take a bath every day, instead of once a week.

• • •

A letter from Barbara in 1993 told me more about the wall hanging made of Chinese coins: "It came from Ah Tai's little store near the Columbia River at Daisy, probably purchased sometime in the 1920s."

In the summer of 1989, I returned to Ella's farmhouse, which Barbara and her husband, Harvey Scott, had turned into a bed-and-breakfast inn. That year the farm was declared a Washington State Centennial Farm, having been homesteaded in 1889 by Barbara's grandparents, William and Mary Carter. More than fifty years later, I remembered the peanut butter cookies, and my eyes wandered to the kitchen counter, expecting the cookie jar to still be there. Barbara gave me her mother's recipe, which I treasure for the memory and the fact that the cookies are delicious.

33

The Outdoor Toilet

I was doing one of my most favorite things: reading. And just I'd just reached an exciting part in my story in *Ranch Romances* magazine, one of the twins tugged at my arm to get my attention. Visions of the... "wiry cowboy racing on a horse to overtake outlaws carrying away his raven-haired sweetheart" ...faded as I looked into the anxious face of my little sister. "Inee," she whimpered, "Have to go pee-pee."

I dropped the magazine and grabbed her small hand, and we hotfooted for the outdoor toilet, about sixty feet away from the house, partially hidden by three lilac bushes.

Not yet two, the twins were scared to sit over the big, round holes of the toilet's bench seat without someone there to watch them. Mom knew it was possible for them to fall through the hole into the pit below, so they had good reason to be afraid. As the oldest girl, I usually was elected to take them on their errand.

While holding onto the twin, I noticed for the umpteenth time how the single layer of rough boards, nailed on vertically, formed the building. The spaces between the boards let in fresh air, which we needed on a hot summer day — as well as the bothersome flies, which no one needed.

Continuing my architectural study of this much-used little house, I saw how the carpenter had chosen a wide board for the seat, long enough to stretch from wall to wall. He had made three big holes at an angle and sanded the edges smooth. Years of use had made them even smoother. Overhead, a single layer of thick cedar shingles covered the small, pitched roof.

Sometimes in nice weather we might dawdle a little while, looking through last year's copy of the Montgomery Ward catalog that served as toilet paper. The pages weren't soft, and we crinkled them up to make them usable — except for the colored pages — no amount of crinkling made them soft.

In summer, the sun baked the roof and raised the inside temperature to over a hundred degrees, making it the hottest place on the farm. The heat was bad enough, but the odor was even worse. Mom dumped lime and wood ashes into the pit but could not get rid of the smell.

Our outdoor toilet was the hottest place in summer and the bitterest cold one in winter. On a frosty, below-zero morning, there was no dawdling over the catalog. The combination of an ice-cold seat and a frigid wind blowing through the cracks hurried us along. At least in winter, there was no bad smell and there were no flies. The toilet was such an unpleasant place that we girls didn't want the men to see us go there. When the threshing crew came to the house to eat, we waited until they had gone back to the field before we headed for the toilet.

Every four or five years the pit filled up, and a new one had to be dug nearby. The toilet was moved into position over the newly dug pit and loose dirt was shoveled into the old one to cover it up. Dad made sure to get this done before Halloween. If news of a full toilet pit got around to some of the boys and young men in our area, it was likely to get tipped over. From overhearing snatches of boys' whispered conversations, I guessed it was a lot of fun. Since nobody would ever admit to having tipped over an outhouse, I couldn't find out for myself.

Even though the farmers kept an ear cocked on Halloween for unusual noises and activities around the outhouse, pranksters occasionally succeeded in tipping over someone's little wooden house. If anyone had come into our yard, the dogs would have alerted Dad, who was all set to scare the pranksters off by shooting his gun into the air.

Finally, Mom got a bright idea of how the twins could go to the toilet all by themselves. She sawed a hole in the floor and nailed the wooden potty chair (made from an apple box) over it. With their feet touching the floor, the twins felt safe and all grown up and able to take care of themselves.

⋙ ⋘

In search of a rest room at a roadside cafe in rural Spain a few years ago, I followed a sign pointing to the *servicio,* which led me outside and around the corner. While in that old-fashioned outhouse, the scene from almost sixty years ago played itself in my memory. I no longer saw the *servicio's* white-painted interior, but the unpainted, weathered-brown boards of the outdoor toilet back on the farm.

Mom and Dad finally got an indoor bathroom after we had grown up and left home.

34

City Relatives

One day when our parents were in town, a strange car drove through our gate; we wondered who could be coming to see us. The car came to a stop in our yard, and a red-headed lady got out. Upon seeing our blank expressions, she asked, "You don't know who we are, do you?"

She was right. We didn't know the three children or the other two grown-ups who had piled out of the car. The red-headed lady looked vaguely familiar, and I had a hunch they could be relatives. It turned out to be Mom's sister-in-law, Lizzie, her sons, and her mother from Lewiston. A friend of Lizzie's mother drove them up in his car.

After Grandma and Charley moved back to Idaho, we had no relatives left in Washington. Dad's brothers and sisters lived in Oregon. Money was scarce, and no one could afford to travel.

Money, or the lack of it, was always the case with our family, and on top of it, we were tied to the demands of our farm with all the daily chores that had to be done. It was no wonder our relatives looked like strangers — it had been years since we'd seen them.

After the brief greetings, we ran out of things to say, other than to answer their questions. Lester and I felt responsible for making them feel welcome, but we hadn't had much practice in talking to strangers. Dad had drilled into us that we had to keep still when grown-ups were visiting. Lizzie had been looking at the steep hill on the far side of our creek, the timbered mountain in the other direction, and the farmland in front of our house. In all that expanse of land, she didn't see another house. "Don't you get lonely here so far away from anyplace?" she asked.

Puzzling about how I could be "far away" when I was living in the very center of my whole world, I replied, "No, I never get lonely. I'm not far away from anything; everything I know is right here."

At long last, our parents drove in, puzzled by just whose car was sitting in the yard. Mom knew who her guests were. Laughing in joyful surprise, she ran to Lizzie and threw her arms around her neck, saying, "Oh, I'm so glad to see you!" Mom's outburst of happiness broke the silence, and suddenly everyone was talking at once. Dad's first question was, "Where's Lester?"

He was disappointed that Lester hadn't been able to come. Uncle Lester had been the one who introduced Dad to Mom years ago. After the grown-ups went into the house, we heard their talk and bursts of laughter. At last released, we launched into our usual country games, and to our surprise, the city kids liked them, too. We raced around the house hollering, using our stored-up energy, and we played ante-I-over, trying to catch the ball as it sailed over the roof. We showed our cousins the barn and blacksmith shop, the horse stalls, and the the cows' stanchions; and Lester explained how things worked on a farm. I showed them the ladder leading up to the square hole in the ceiling and explained that it led to the hay mow, from where we fork hay down into the manger so the cows can eat while they were being milked.

We went to the creek behind the barn where the cattle drank. We had a look at the pigs in the pigpen and the chickens. We liked taking our visitors on a tour of the farm, and they seemed interested in everything. Two days later, when our relatives left, we hated to see them go. The "red-headed lady" and the other strangers had become part of our family.

The following year, and just as unexpectedly, two of Mom's brothers, Elmo and Bob Dryden, drove up from Lewiston in their Model-A Ford. Mom had filled our heads full of stories about taking care of her four younger brothers, and she was more than happy to to see them.

Usually our men visitors pitched in to help with the outside chores. But that first night when Dad and Lester headed for the barn to milk, Elmo and Bob stayed to visit with their sister, who had been more like a mother to them and whom they hadn't seen for a long time. Early the next morning, our uncles went to the barn to do chores, and Elmo offered to lend a hand at digging postholes for a fence Dad was building.

Mom was going to bake bread, and she sifted flour into the big aluminum dishpan while her brother Bob looked on. I was surprised to see a man helping in the kitchen — and obviously enjoying it. Although all the girls and Mom did many outside chores and fieldwork, Dad and Lester never helped us with the cooking or housework.

Bob asked Mom to bake maple bars, and they shaped the remaining dough into bars and placed them on a greased baking sheet. She made a powdered sugar icing, adding maple flavoring, spreading it on the bars when they had cooled.

That night at the supper table, Elmo said the magic words, "Do you remember ...?" and off the four grown-ups went, recalling the past and talking about events that had happened before any of us were born. They remembered the cheat-grass fire that Frank had started accidentally when his car's hot exhaust pipe set the dry grass on fire when he bounced over the rough ground. The blaze ate its way uphill as everyone stood by helplessly. Fortunately, the fire ran only a short distance before coming to a rockslide. With no more grass to feed on, the fire died out.

Mom's brothers lived around the Lewiston area — about a two-hundred- mile drive away. But Dad's brothers and sisters lived much farther away, in Oregon. We were surprised when his younger brother, Elmer, with his wife Ruth and their three girls, showed up. The brothers also hadn't seen each other in years.

When Dad recognized the stranger who had pulled his car into the yard, a big grin spread across his face. He grabbed Elmer's hand and pumped it. "By grab," he said, "it's sure as hell good to see you!" Mom took her visitors in the house while Dad admired every inch of his brother's shiny gray car, feeling the smoothness of the Chevrolet's unblemished body and flawless interior. He turned to his brother and exclaimed in wonder, "I've never had a new car, but this looks brand new to me. You must have just bought it!"

Shyly, Elmer replied "Yes, I did. I wanted to try it out on a trip. We drove over seven hundred and fifty miles from Ashland, Oregon, and it didn't give us a lick of trouble."

Lester, Dora and I were glad to meet more cousins — more people who belonged to us. And, like we did with our other cousins, we wanted to show them our favorite view from the top of the hill, where we could see the mountains clear across the Columbia River and the top of Monumental Mountain.

As we walked up the wagon road, I told our cousins about the spring flowers and how we looked for lavender Mariposa lilies that open up in the summer, how we might come across a deer in the grainfield. Chattering away in our excitement to show them our favorite places, we hadn't noticed the girls' lack of interest. Their pretty dresses and nice shoes weren't suited for a tour of of the countryside on foot. Disappointed, we turned around and went back to the house without having seen anything.

Exploring the hills appeared to be a shock to our city cousins. They were probably more accustomed to cutting out paper dolls or coloring in books. They had probably never played with tomboys who liked following in their big brother's footsteps.

A couple of days later, I regretfully watched as Uncle Elmer and our cousins drove out of the yard. My eyes followed the car until it went out of sight below the mailboxes at the junction. I couldn't help but wonder what games these town girls liked; we had never bothered to find out.

All the relatives who visited us seemed to enjoy their stay. They commented on the clean, fresh mountain air, and not getting their fill of the cool, sweet spring water.

As much as the other member of the family expressed their fondness for "Bill and Sis" and certain things about our valley, they knew there weren't any jobs to be had or ways to make a living. For Aunt Lizzie, it was a"lonely place, being so far away," without electricity or indoor plumbing, which came with town living. Somehow, we sensed they wouldn't trade places.

35

Target Practice

Our father was a good shot, and whenever he needed to adjust his rifle sight, Dora and I took the cardboard target Leola and Effie had drawn, ran through the barnyard, crossed the creek, and climbed about twenty-five feet up the hill. We propped the target against some rocks, about a hundred yards from where Dad was sitting — a good test distance for sighting-in the rifle — and away from the livestock. Back on the porch we watched as Dad steadied the long barrel on the back of a wooden chair in front of him.

He pulled the butt firmly up to his left shoulder, hunching down, until his jaw pressed against the wood. Pulling back the hammer with his thumb and holding the front sight deep in the notch of the rear sight, he aimed at the middle of the bull's eye. Slowly he squeezed the trigger. The sudden loud boom made me jump, even though I was expecting it.

No matter how many times I watched him shoot a rifle from close by, I always reacted to the noise, and I was always surprised to see him shooting left-handed when he did everything else right-handed. Leola and Effie raced to get the target so he could see how well he had done. Noting the bullet hole five inches above the bull's eye, he exclaimed, "Hell, it's no wonder I missed that deer. I shot right over its head!"

He adjusted the rear sight and continued shooting and adjusting the sight until he put a bullet hole right in the middle of the bull's eye. He was all set for his next hunting trip.

In the summer of 1936, when Lester was fourteen and I was twelve, we had plenty of our own target practice. But instead of using a paper target, we shot at ground squirrels with .22-caliber rifles.

The grayish-brown ground squirrels were a nuisance because they dug holes in the grainfields and in the grazing land, piling the loose dirt up in high mounds around their holes. During the cutting of hay and grain, the sickles of the mowing machine and binder rammed into the dirt piles, which would dull the sickles' teeth and even break them. The squirrel holes were also a hazard for the horses, who could easily break a leg if they stepped into one of the holes. Dad was all for our target practice and kept us supplied with .22-caliber shells.

We never ran out of targets. The squirrels multiplied faster than we could kill them. We became quite adept at handling rifles and learned to be careful so we wouldn't shoot anyone. And by learning to shoot straight, we even earned a few nickels and dimes.

During that time the government paid a bounty of two cents for each squirrel. We would turn in the tails of our targets to the Stevens County Extension and collect the bounty. Even though each tin box of squirrel tails seldom earned more than fifty cents, it gave us some spending money we wouldn't have had otherwise, and kept us interested in our job.

One of our rifles was just a single-shot, while the other had a clip that held six bullets. Since Lester was the oldest, he got first dibs on the better gun, and I had to be content with using the single-shot. I didn't get to shoot the repeating rifle until he left home a few years later. By that time, Dora was old enough to learn to shoot, and she inherited the single-shot.

It wasn't hard to find our targets. All we had to do was look for the mounds of dirt the squirrels had thrown up digging their holes and sit down and wait for one to come up. They made good targets when they stood up on their hind legs to look around.

Just about that time, *The Washington Farmer*, a monthly magazine, sponsored a photography contest. I got Leola and Effie to pose for me. They sat on a little rise in the front yard and held their guns crossed in front of them in the shape of an "X". Buster, our big German Shepherd, with his ears pointed, sat on his haunches behind them.

We were surprised at how nice the picture turned out. I sent it in to the magazine contest and forgot about it. A couple of months later, Ike Cranston, the mail carrier, left a letter from *The Washington Farmer* addressed to us in our mailbox. There was a check for five dollars inside the envelope, along with a letter saying I'd won a prize! Their next issue listed my name as one of the photo contest winners. I was thrilled with my prize and with getting my name in the magazine to boot.

Part of the money Lester earned from turning in squirrel tails bought him his first pocketwatch. One day, when he heard me volunteer to go to all the way to the Rice store for Mom, he handed me a silver dollar and said, "Ines, bring me one of those Ingersoll pocketwatches." I rounded up Betty, bridled her, and rode out our gate, with my old denim lunch bag hanging around my neck. It would come in handy for carrying things home from the store.

About a half-hour later, I rode past the Rice Community Church and down into the curving, tree-shaded dip where the road crossed Quillisascut Creek. After topping a slight rise, the few buildings making up the town of Rice came into view: two white houses; the two-story, false-fronted Clinton Mercantile Store; a square, two-story brown house, where my favorite dance partner, Leroy Small, lived; the post office and the Odd Fellows Hall. I passed the house where Vivian Rice, a friend my age, lived, and remembered that Rice was named after Vivian's grandparents, William and Mary Rice, the first white settlers in the area.

At the store, I slid off Betty's back, tied her to a white picket fence, brushed off the horsehair that clung to my sweaty pants from my long bareback ride, and entered the crowded store. Horsecollars hung from long nails, and harnesses draped and looped from nail to nail on one wall like curtains. On the wooden floor, golden spools of binder twine sat in neat stacks, their pungent odor mingling with that of coiled new ropes and the oil-stained boards of the floor. Canned goods, sugar, flour, cereal, a few loaves of bread, and other staples filled the big rack in the center aisle and were stacked on low shelves against the walls.

The big cash register that sat on top of a large glass case fascinated me. It had shiny buttons and something magic inside that rang a bell every time the cash drawer was opened. When Mr. Clinton set the items Mom needed on the counter, I handed him the money, and he pushed several of the cash register's buttons and gave the crank a couple of turns. The bell dinged and the drawer flew open. I handed him Lester's silver dollar and, pointing to the display in the glass case, saying, "And Lester wants one of those Ingersoll pocket watches."

Mr. Clinton smiled as he slid open the big glass door on his side of the counter, reached inside, and brought out a square white cardboard box. He lifted out a round watch with a big stem on top and proceeded to show me how to wind it and set the time. The cash register performed its magic one more time, Mr. Clinton plunked the heavy dollar in the open drawer, then pushed it shut. I put the watch in the bottom of my denim bag, under the box of brown sugar, for safekeeping, untied Betty's rope, and headed home.

Dad's early lessons in target practice taught us gun safety, and made us feel at ease with guns. He taught us their proper care and handling, cautioning, "Don't ever point a gun at anyone, and always act as if a gun is fully loaded, even if you've just emptied it."

We were never tempted to play with the loaded rifles that stood behind the kitchen door. We enjoyed our target practice and knew we were accomplishing something by thinning out the squirrel population. Learning to shoot straight offered us the added opportunity to earn a little spending money, which didn't hurt our feelings either.

36

My Fourteenth Birthday

In the afternoon of March 14, 1938, Lester and I set out with a couple of milk buckets to get some snow. It was my fourteenth birthday, and we needed the snow to make ice cream to go with the birthday cake. Snow had melted everywhere, except for a patch under the low-hanging limbs of a thickly branched cedar. We skimmed off the winter's accumulation of dirt and scooped up the glistening, clear white crystals underneath.

By the time we carried our two buckets of snow back to the house, Mom had the ice cream mixture ready. She had beaten several eggs, added sugar and vanilla, and poured it into the freezer can, added enough thick cream to fill the two-gallon can, and closed the lid. We all liked vanilla ice cream and never thought of making any other flavor.

Lester put some of the snow into the outer wooden part of the freezer and settled the can of mix down into it. After packing more snow around the sides, he fitted the heavy metal gear mechanism on, fastening the clamp to the top of the freezer, and turned the handle. The paddles whirled the mix around so that all of it touched the icy can and eventually froze. It was something like churning butter but getting ice cream instead.

Usually Mom didn't have time to give us kids much attention, what with all the heavy work she had to do, but on our birthdays she took time to make us feel important. We seldom received a birthday present, so the one I received for my fourteenth birthday was extra special.

After we had eaten our cake and ice cream, Mom handed me a paper sack. I upended the sack and slowly pulled out a beautiful blue cotton dress with a large white accordion-pleated organdy collar. I couldn't help exclaiming, "It's beautiful; now I have something special to wear to the next dance!"

I tried it on immediately. It was perfect. I'd been growing so fast that nothing seemed long enough for my five-foot, seven-inch height. Mom looked at me and said, "You look nice. Let's go outside so I can take a picture."

• • •

It was one of the best birthdays I'd ever had. I felt pampered, not only in having a beautiful new dress, but also for having had my own special day that included getting my picture taken. Even making the ice cream had been fun.

Of the nine birthdays we celebrated, I felt mine was the luckiest one, coming as it did in mid-March, just in time to make ice cream one last time before the snow all melted.

37

The Garner Place

Soon after we had moved to the Home Place, Dad rented the farm across the road from us for less than a hundred dollars a year. The new addition of land brought us extra pasture for the cows, a spot for a big vegetable garden, a neglected old orchard, and about twenty acres that Dad planted in oats. Although we called it the Garner Place, it was really government land on which the Garner family had a long-term lease. When they moved out of the country, they rented the farm to us.

Almost a mile northeast of our house, the Garner house stood on a bench of land part way up Monumental Mountain in the Huckleberry Mountain Range. From our garden, we could see several wooded hills to the south — snuggled against the hills rising toward Carter Canyon. We watched cars grind slowly up the steep grade of the Folsom Hill, as they shifted into low gear on their climb up the long hill.

Behind the Garner house, the top of Monumental Mountain rose 5,500 feet into the blue sky, looking beautiful in the clear sunlight. At dusk the rounded peaks made a dark outline against the sky. Cedar, pine, tamarack, fir and quaking aspen trees partially covered the mountain, and chaparral, buck brush, serviceberry, thimbleberry and other greenery grew everywhere. In the draws the growth was quite dense, but on the rounded sides of the mountain there were several openings between the trees, making it easy to spot deer.

The seasons gave the mountain different looks, and each one was beautiful. In the winter, covered with snow, the mountain was just as beautiful as it was in the fall when the aspen and tamarack turned gold, making bright splashes against the dark greens of the firs and pines. It was a quiet and peaceful place. The air was clear except when a forest fire's bluish haze dimmed the far mountains.

Before we used the Garner Place, we grew a garden near our big front gate but had gotten tired of trying to coax water across an almost-level spot to irrigate the rows of vegetables. The Garner Place had better soil and was irrigated by a ditch fed from a spring on the mountain. The runoff water from the garden seeped into the pasture, watering about a quarter of an acre of grass. In late summer the pasture grass stayed green, providing a refreshingly cool contrast to the bleached white grass beyond it. Nearby a few neglected apple, cherry and prune trees still bore fruit, and beyond this old orchard a brushy slope fell abruptly to a grainfield. Below the field a steep bank plunged down to the dirt road separating our two farms.

In the spring Dad had plowed up a quarter of an acre of ground near the Garner house. Mom took over with her hoe, binder twine wrapped around sticks for making straight rows, and all her little packets of seeds. We all helped her plant our vegetable garden. We put in green beans, peas, beets, carrots, turnips, radishes, lettuce, Swiss chard and onion sets.

Since this garden was so far from our house, getting there was as much work as the planting and hoeing. Long before vegetables were ready, we had walked back and forth many times. We planted our tender tomato plants near our house, where they weren't so apt to get nipped by late frosts that came to the higher elevation at the Garner Place. We planted our dry beans, potatoes, and sweet corn near our grainfields, because they could do without irrigation.

One day, as I was weeding with my sisters, an unexpected excitement took the drudgery out of our work for a moment. After climbing the last hill, we looked up at the old house and saw a steer sticking his head out the upstairs window. No one had lived in the house for some time, and most of the windows and doors were missing. We knew that cattle had wandered in and out of the abandoned house by the manure piles they left behind. What we didn't know was that cows climbed stairs!

We knew we should try to get the steer back down the stairs. After much puzzling and discussing the situation, we decided to sneak through the doorway, somehow get around behind him, and shoo him down the stairs.

It didn't work that way. The old steer saw us when we got to the top of the stairs, didn't wait for our next move, and plunged out the window. We raced down the stairs, expecting to see him lying splat on the ground with a broken leg or two. But when we got there, he was walking away on four good legs as if he jumped out of a second-story window every day.

My earliest memories of the Garner Place went back to when I was about four years old, when we visited Grandma and her husband, Charley. It was about dinnertime and Grandma was tending to a hot stove, frying up some steaks, when a car pulled into the yard and four strangers piled out.

Showing their badges to Dad and Charley, who had gone to meet the men, the strangers announced they were game wardens. One of them addressed Charley, saying that someone reported that he'd been killing deer out of season. The game wardens wanted to check the barn and other buildings.

Charley and Dad watched while the men searched the barn, the bunkhouse, the chicken house, the shop and the woodshed. While they were busily looking in all the possible hiding places, Grandma was frying up the last of the venison steaks.

About twenty minutes later, the game wardens came to the house empty-handed. Grandma invited the game wardens to join us for supper. The strangers sat down at the table, obviously enjoyed the steaks, thanked Grandma for the good meal, got back into their car, and drove away. Since there was no evidence of Charley killing deer out of season, the game wardens couldn't very well haul him off to jail. As they drove out of the yard, Dad remarked, "By grab, Charley, they knew all along they were eating deer meat. They just didn't want to arrest you for killing a deer to feed your family."

In addition to the cows that pastured on the Garner Place, Dad also grazed some sheep. When he discovered to his dismay that a bear had killed a few lambs, he took his large beartrap — the one with big teeth in its jaws — to the orchard, opened its menacing jaws as far as they'd go, set the trap, and anchored it to a prune tree with a heavy chain.

Several evenings later, he went out to check the trap, taking his rifle. When he arrived at the orchard, there was the bear all right, but it wasn't trapped the way Dad had envisioned it. The big animal was sitting smack-dab in the middle of the open trap, eating prunes that had fallen off the tree. Dad raised his rifle, took aim, and shot the bear sitting in the trap. We had bear meat for a few weeks instead of venison, and Dad had another bearskin to tan.

After planting a garden at the Garner Place for three years, Dad decided to give it up and make a garden spot at our house, despite the poor soil and irrigation problems. We were relieved we wouldn't have to make that long hike uphill every time the beans or peas needed picking, or when it was time to hoe weeds.

38

Logging Camp
Adventures

Jo and Roy Naff were the last people to live in the Garner house before it became rundown and deserted. Roy was logging off the big pine and fir trees in the section next to it and had brought Jo along to cook. While we rented the farm, we never had any use for the house, and Roy used it as a headquarters for his logging operations.

I'd been helping Jo cook for the loggers — after all, I was fourteen and had been Mom's right hand for years. One day Jo had to go to town for supplies and left me in charge of the noonday meal. She had put a beef roast in the oven, and all I had to do was fix some potatoes, make gravy, open some green beans, and wash the strawberries.

I was determined to have dinner ready when the men quit at noon and got to work as soon as Jo left. By the time the loggers took their noon break, I had the table set and the food ready. I quickly sliced the roast, dished up the beans, potatoes and gravy, and put them on the table along with bread, butter and glasses of water. When the men came inside from washing, steam was still rising from the platters and serving bowls. Suddenly I panicked. I realized I'd forgotten to wash the strawberries for dessert. I felt like a failure.

I hurriedly began to wash the berries when Fred Wooley, the logging-truck driver, who noticed how flustered I was, got up from the table and pitched in. This big, friendly man stood beside me, washing and stemming each berry with his big fingers just as carefully as I did. The other loggers continued eating, glancing sideways at us from time to time. Few men ever helped in the kitchen, and I wondered if they'd razz Fred later about doing woman's work. If he hadn't already been one of the men I liked best, he would have become my favorite instantly.

I was glad Dad had gone home to eat dinner that day and wasn't eating with the rest of the crew. Always wanting him to be proud of me, I would have been even more embarrassed if he'd seen dinner wasn't completely ready when the crew arrived.

Although Dad had officially left the logging business, he still went back to it at times to earn extra money. After he planted his spring grain, there wasn't that much to do on the farm until the winter wheat was ready to be harvested. He worked logging jobs with his friend, Louie Koerner, who had an old logging truck and hired out to haul logs from the woods to the sawmill. Felling those giant trees took two men using a crosscut saw, and the job wasn't any easier than it had been twenty years ago.

Dad operated the log jammer, which was a big, noisy engine with a winch that skidded logs from where the sawyers felled them to a loading area, then lifted them onto the dual-carriage truck. Logging was strenuous work, and the workday started shortly after daylight.

Occasionally, Mom came up with the five girls. I joined them, and we walked to the site where the men worked, and watched the operation from a safe distance. The air was filled with the pungent smells of freshly crushed pine and fir needles. Our shoes, scuffing the loose dirt, released a damp, earthy smell which mingled with that of the evergreens and piles of yellowish-white sawdust around newly cut stumps. We saw a bulldozer butt its way through the brush, push over small trees, and gouge out a new track for the truck to get through. Just seeing the big trees get cut down and loaded was exciting.

As we approached the logging site, we could hear the sound of a crosscut saw, the warning shouts, and finally the solid thump of a tree falling heavily to the ground. Soon there was the sound of the bucker chopping limbs off the tree with his sharp, double-bitted axe.

Cutting down these big trees took skill and a lot of muscle. We watched as two men approached a big fir which was at least ten feet wide at its base. To make the tree fall in a certain direction, the men had to make a notch on that side of the trunk. Each took hold of one of the wooden handles on their huge saws and, placing the teeth of the saw next to the bark and made a short, slanting cut. They finished chopping out the notch with an axe and went to the opposite side to saw toward the notch.

We stood fixed to the ground in thrilled expectation as the saw went in deeper and deeper. Just before the saw reached the notch, the tip of the tree started to tremble, ready to fall. The sawyers glanced up and took another pull with the saw, and when the tip began to sway, they quickly drew the saw out of the cut, yelled, "T-I-M-B-E-R," and jumped quickly to one side. The big tree came crashing down, breaking limbs off other trees in its fall, and slammed into the ground with a thundering roar.

After resting for a moment, the two men picked up their axes and headed for the giant fallen tree. They climbed onto the tree trunk, the sharp caulks in the boot soles keeping them from slipping off, and began cutting the limbs off flush with the trunk. That done, they measured the correct lengths for logs and marked them with chalk where they needed to saw.

Another day when we hadn't gone to the logging site, the men had a little excitement while chopping limbs off the fallen trees. One of the sawyers carried kerosene to pour on his saw when it got sticky with pitch. The glass container, a flat pint whiskey bottle, just fit into his back pocket. As he was walking on top of a downed tree chopping off tree limbs, his caulked boots caught on the stub of a limb and he fell flat on the trunk, landing on his backside and breaking the bottle. Pieces of glass lodged in his rear end.

Two of the other loggers helped the injured man down to the barn, put him face down on a blanket, and picked out the broken glass from the injured man's rear. Unfortunately the cut was so big it needed to be sewn up. One of the men came into the house and told Jo what had happened and that someone had gone down to Ernie Keck's to telephone a doctor in Colville. They asked Jo for a clean cloth to cover the wound. She hunted up a white cloth and gave it to him. Having heard only bits of the whispered conversation, I wanted to know the whole story and told Jo I was going to see what was going on. I hadn't heard enough to know a man was lying in the barn with no pants on because of a gash in his butt. She stopped me by saying, "That's no place for a girl right now."

The loggers who bunked at the Garner Place spent their free time playing cards. One of them had brought an unusual toy from his Southern homeland — a jointed, wooden doll. A simple connection on its back made it hang suspended over a slat. He showed us how he could make the doll dance by hitting the slat with his hand. The doll swung its arms and clacked its feet against the board, clogging and clattering while the logger accompanied it by singing in a high-pitched twangy voice. Leola and Effie were enthralled, and asked him to make the doll dance again and again.

Just before the end of the logging operations, the hooker quit, leaving Roy Naff in the lurch. Unable to find a replacement on short notice, Dad took on the job, on top of running the jammer. He would have to pick up the heavy tongs, pull the wire cable downhill from the jammer to the log, hook the tongs, then climb back uphill — fighting his way through brush and over rocks — to the jammer to snake the log up and load it on the waiting truck. As always, with a big family to feed, he wanted to make the extra money.

But strong as he was, he couldn't do the work of two men without wearing himself out. Every day he came home dog tired, dragging his feet, and went to bed right after supper. Mom scolded him, saying, "That extra money isn't worth killing yourself for."

My parents were relieved when the logging operations were completed.

Cooking for a logging crew taught me a few things and was an adventure. Jo Naff was easy to work for, the work hadn't been hard, and I had earned some money. But I, too, was glad when the logging ended, and I no longer had to walk up to the Garner Place every day. I had also missed being part of the daytime family life, and all of us were glad to see that summer's logging adventures come to an end.

Grandma

We could always tell when Mom was getting homesick for her mother and brothers in Idaho. Loneliness sounded in her voice when she talked about caring for her younger brothers from the time she was five years old; about Uncle Lester buying her a new coat; about Buster and Elmo playing boyish tricks on her, and about Frank and Bob tagging along when she went walking with her first boyfriend.

Most of Mom's relatives lived in or near Lewiston, which seemed far away. In the midst of the Depression, two hundred miles might just as well be two thousand. Besides, we had cows to milk twice a day and there was no extra money for a trip. We couldn't go visit relatives no matter how lonesome anyone was.

Just before Thanksgiving one year, Mom worried about Grandma —wondering if she'd be able to buy a turkey. Since

Charley had deserted her and their two young sons, she existed on county welfare checks and what little money her married sons could contribute. But times were hard for everyone; the young men could barely make ends meet and were unable to help a whole lot.

Mom was still trying to figure out just how she could help, when she glanced out the window toward the granary and saw our chickens pecking and scratching at the grain on the ground. Her face lit up. We didn't have any money to send Grandma to buy a turkey, and we didn't have one to send — but we did have chickens.

A few days before the holiday, Mom killed and dressed out two good-sized chickens and hung them outside overnight in the bitter cold weather. The next morning they were frozen stiff. She wrapped them in several thicknesses of newspaper, put them in a large cardboard box, and Dad made a special trip to Kettle Falls to mail the frozen chickens.

The chickens reached Grandma a couple of days later, and her Thanksgiving dinner was still cold and fresh. Mom was pleased that she had figured out how to give Grandma roast chickens for the holiday.

After Grandma had moved from Pleasant Valley, we didn't see much of her. In summer, she rode the bus to visit us and stayed about a month. She told us all kinds of things, and shared her home remedies, including those for preventing wrinkles and gray hair. She believed that in order to prevent wrinkles, you should splash your face with cold water first thing in the morning, then wash it in warm water. It must have worked for Grandmother, because at fifty-seven she didn't have many wrinkles. But we didn't think much of her remedy of using sagebrush tea on her hair to keep it from going gray. The tea didn't help, it just made her hair stink.

Grandma made her own sage tea by breaking the branches into short pieces, and simmering them in a pan of water for almost an hour. As soon as the water boiled, the sagebrush turned the water brown, and the odor was enough to make us wish she'd be happy with gray hair. When she considered the tea to be ready for use, she combed the stinky liquid through her hair. It smelled awful, and we steered clear of her for at least an hour.

Another of Grandma's remedies was made from chittam bark tea. Convinced kids should have a good physic about every two weeks, she made us take some of the bitter liquid whether we needed it or not. Grandma brought her own supply of bark with her and made the tea by simmering chittam (cascara) tree bark in water. We took it, but only under protest.

But the day I got my first permanent wave, I was glad to have Grandma with me. It was in the fall of 1938, just before Lester and I started our freshman year at Kettle Falls High School. Mom knew how excited I was about starting high school, and how I'd always wanted to have curly hair. She told me I could have the money to get a permanent wave. Grandma and I caught a ride with Dad to Kettle Falls, where there was a beauty parlor.

I hadn't realized that getting a permanent was such a complicated process. The hairdresser cut and washed my hair, parted it into sections, and rolled it on long, skinny rods, pulling so tight it felt like she was going to pull my hair out by the roots. She seated me in a chair which had an odd-looking contraption hovering above that dangled electrical cords with clamps at each end. The thing reminded me of an octopus. As the operator attached a clamp over each of the rods, my head became heavier and heavier. When all the rods had clamps covering them, the load was so heavy, my neck felt it was supporting a ten-pound sack of sugar.

My neck got tired and stiff, and I thought the twenty minutes it took to process the permanent wave would never end. But when the rods came out, my hair was all curly. The operator finished the job with a strong-smelling rinse, rolled my hair up in curlers, and put me under a cone-shaped machine which blew hot air on my head, drying my hair a lot faster than the sun. After the operator brushed out my hair, Grandma kept touching it in admiration, saying, "My, don't you look nice with curly hair!" That made me feel so good, I silently forgave her for all the chittam bark tea she'd made me drink.

Getting a professional permanent wave was a lot better than what I had done to my hair in an experiment. I had read somewhere that curly hair had flat cells and straight hair had round cells. I decided that if I pounded on my hair with something heavy, it would flatten out those darned round cells and maybe my hair would curl. The best thing I could think of was Dad's anvil. Bending over the anvil, I laid a lock of long hair over it and gave it a few good whacks with the ballpeen hammer. Then I ran my hand over that length to see if I could feel any difference. My hair did not turn curly, but I discovered chunks of hair that had broken off with my pounding and now littered the rough wooden floorboards. My experiment had been a failure. I was stuck with round cells and straight hair — until that magic day I had my permanent wave.

Grandma belonged to the Seventh-Day-Adventist Church and was thankful to the Lord for her daily existence. She would say a lengthy blessing before supper. We had never said grace at mealtime and were not happy with Grandma changing our routine. We complained to Mom, grumbling about having to wait so long before we could eat. She shushed us, saying, "It won't hurt you to wait a few minutes."

But Grandma's ways soon caused a strain between Dad and Mom. It was plain to see Dad didn't think much of the long-winded blessings. Several times he endured them politely, sitting and fidgeting while Grandma went through her long list of "thank-yous." But one day he got tired of waiting for the end of the blessing, picked up his fork, and started eating before she said, "Amen."

From then on, she just bowed her head and asked a silent blessing. Sitting across from her, I couldn't help seeing her bowed head and closed eyes. Even though we had grumbled about waiting, it now seemed impolite to start eating, and Mom was the only one who waited. Dad's unwillingness to be patient while Grandma asked the blessing puzzled me. He and Mom lived by the Golden Rule and the Ten Commandments. Although his everyday speech had plenty of "dammit-all-to-Hells" and "sonsabitches" sprinkled through it, he thought it was unforgivable if someone stole, lied, cheated or went back on his word. He didn't like or trust anyone who was guilty of that. He was what people called "a square shooter."

Dad expected everyone to keep his word. If he promised something, he'd almost die before he broke that promise. Many times he told us that a man's word was his bond. He and other farmers seldom had written contracts in dealing with each other and relied on a handshake instead of a piece of paper.

At the end of her visit, Grandma caught the bus back to Lewiston, taking what was left of her chittam bark. In some ways, we weren't sorry to see her go and settled back into our routine minus the silent blessings, sagebrush and chittam bark teas.

By the time Grandma visited us two summers later, I had learned to type. Happy to hear this, she said, "Oh, good. You can set down my life story on paper as I tell it to you and write down the history of my parents and grandparents!" She went on to say, "I've seen many changes in the settling of the country. We moved from one farm to another in a covered wagon, and now almost everyone drives a car. I've had more than my share of hardships, and I wish you could write it all down for me."

I would like to have done it for Grandma, but we couldn't afford to buy a typewriter, and I didn't think the high school would let me borrow one of their Underwoods. So we never got her life story "set down" on paper.

However, Mom told us bits and pieces about her mother's life. She told us how Grandma grew up in dire poverty and hardship. As the oldest of ten children, she was still little when she had to help with housework and the care of her younger sisters and brothers. Without electricity or running water in their house, everything was done the hard way, including scrubbing clothes on the washboard.

Grandma got lonely, too, and often wrote two-page letters to us. She seldom used periods. Sometimes her letters consisted of only one paragraph. Despite that, and her misspelled words, we were able to figure out what she meant.

One of her letters went: "My dearest children, one and all, Why in the Devil don't some of you take time to write to an old guy like me look and look for a letter an none comes this makes three letters I have written an I guess you did answer one of them I do hope this finds you all well an at work but haying over isn't it but soon will be time to can corn an are you going to dry some an how I like to have some …

Love to all. XXX 000 XXX 000 XXX
Mary M. Adams"

❧   ❦

Grandma spent her last years in Lewiston. She died August 8, 1946, at the age of 65.; A broken rib had penetrated her lung. Death released her from a life of pain, poverty and hardship.

Grandma was the only grandparent we ever knew. We never met our father's parents. Hard times, with its shortage of money, had kept the family from visiting each other. His father, Peter Riley, died in 1921 in Madras, Oregon, before Lester was born. His mother, Dora Wheeler Riley, died in Idaho in 1925, the year after I was born.

In later years, when Uncle Lester was telling about all of Grandma's husbands, he said, "My father, George Steeley, treated

Mother better than any of her other husbands, but he went to the store one day and just didn't come back."

I still have the envelope to Grandma's letter dated August 8, 1945, and it bears a three-cent "Iwo Jima" stamp. When I read her letter, I can again smell the pungent sagebrush tea in her hair, hear her querulous — yet caring — voice, and see her gaunt frame stooping to pick up kindling. And I think of the Sunbonnet Girl quilt she gave me, and marvel at how hard she worked to appliqué all those flowered dresses and sunbonnets. I've handed down the heirloom to my daughter, Janet Eileen, to put her in touch with her Great-Grandmother Mary Margaret Denney Adams.

40

Getting Ready
for the Threshing Crew

Our new John Deere binder sat gleaming in the bright sun. It sure was a beauty, with its shiny green and yellow paint and the varnished wooden arms poised, waiting to begin their job of pushing the standing grain against the sickle. In its shining newness, the machine looked bigger than our old, rusty binder — held together with baling wire, its weary wooden arms sagging from hard use — which Dad had struggled to keep running for the past five years.

Dad had checked the readiness of the wheat and reported his findings. "When I broke a head and rubbed it in my palms, it shelled out easily. Why, the chaff practically jumped off the grains of wheat! I'll start binding tomorrow morning."

Lester and Dad harnessed our four biggest horses and hitched them to the new binder. It was a heavy piece of machinery and would take our four strongest horses to operate. Sitting squarely on the binder's contoured and perforated metal seat, Dad held the long leather reins and drove the horses as they pulled the binder up the steep grade and into the first grainfield. Lester, Dora and I followed on foot to shock the grain bundles.

About three weeks earlier, Dad had cut a couple of swaths around the field with the mowing machine and made room for the binder to work without knocking down the grain. The still-green grain had already been gathered up in the wagon and taken to the barn for the cows and horses.

As soon as Dad got the binder next to the grain, he put it into gear. The revolving arms reached about halfway down on the stalks, pushing them against the sickle on the edge of the binder bed. The sickle glided back and forth under the guards, cutting the stalks, which fell onto the moving canvas bed, which in turn took them up into the binder. There they were gathered into tight bundles and wrapped securely with twine. The curved needle was a blur as it darted in and out to tie the bundles. A knife cut the twine, and a lever automatically kicked the bundle out to a carrying basket. When it had four or five bundles in it, Dad tripped another lever and the bundles dropped to the ground.

We followed along behind, picking up the bundles to make shocks. We jabbed the first two bundles hard into the stubble, propping them upright against each other. We put six to eight bundles in each shock and placed two bundles across the top to help keep out the rain. Dad worked alone on the binder, cutting the grain. Lester, Dora and I shocked all of it by ourselves. It was hard work, but we managed to joke around, which made it a bit more fun. When the work was done, we felt good, having contributed our share to bringing in the harvest.

After that part of the wheat harvest was over, Dad didn't worry quite so much about bad weather damaging the crop, yet he never completely relaxed until the threshing was done and the grain was safely stored in the granary.

Stacked and stored, the crop represented several seasons of hard work, from preparing the fields for planting, to the planting itself, and finally the harvest. So much of our livelihood depended on a good harvest. The Depression had affected everyone, and farmers were no exception. Everyone pitched in to bring in the crop. We were proud about having done our part.

The Threshing Crew

About the same time each year, Dad announced, "The threshers are coming!" and got everyone's immediate attention. But that summer of 1938, we heard the throbbing of the tractor's engine reverberating up the valley, long before the men arrived.

Looking beyond our mailbox at the junction of the Pleasant Valley Road, we glimpsed the tall threshing machine being pulled by the big tractor, trailed by the crew, in two pick-up trucks. Creeping along, its engine roaring, the tractor soon pulled into our yard and stopped at the house, cutting the noisy engine back to idle. Together, the threshing machine and tractor looked almost as big as our house. After the tractor pulled into the field of shocked grain, the men fitted all the parts into their working positions. The long spout at the top would blow straw out onto the ground, creating a

straw stack. The shorter pipe would funnel grain into the gunnysacks hooked onto the ends of the double pipe.

Besides being big and noisy, the tractor vibrated and made me
think of a giant rust-colored frog squatting on the ground, huffing
and puffing, breathing hard, its sides heaving. Even idling, the
tractor seemed to swell up as it continued throbbing and chugging.
The racket almost drowned out Dad's words as he told the driver to
follow him to the grainfields.

By that time, most of the threshing crew had arrived, bringing
their own teams and hay wagons. Paul Holter would come later,
because there wouldn't be any grain to haul until after the thresher
was set up and a wagonload of bundles hauled to it.

Paul was a lot of fun because he liked to get into water fights
with us. He was our closest neighbor and traded work with Dad
during threshing. He hauled the threshed grain down the hill to the
granary, and in between loads he joked and played games with us
and had just as much fun as we did. That was why we plotted to
have a water fight with him.

Setting out two washtubs in the yard near his wagon route, we
filled the tubs with cold water, watched the road beyond the barn,
and when we saw him, we ran back into the house so he wouldn't
suspect anything. We waited until he had emptied the grain into the
bins and turned the wagon around. As he drove past the house, we
ran out to the tubs and threw water at him. Whooping with delight
and dripping water, Paul stopped his team, wrapped the reins
around a post at the front of the wagon and jumped down, all in one
motion. Red faced with laughter, he grabbed an empty bucket and
drenched all four of us girls in one throw. We, too, got a good
cooling off.

Our water fights went on all afternoon, starting anew each
time Paul brought a load down. Mom stood at the window
laughing, enjoying them as much as we did. We thought Paul was

lucky — he was the only one of the threshing crew who got cooled off on that hot day. The men working and sweating around the threshing machine with chaff sticking to their bodies and blowing down their necks would have liked to change places with him.

Threshing was much more exciting than the rest of the farmwork, and we looked forward eagerly to every year. Dad enjoyed joking and laughing with the men, whom he didn't see often during the summer when everyone was busy with the crops. Having the crew at our farm meant a change in the everyday routine for all of us. For us kids, it promised excitement, but for Mom, it guaranteed more hard work with all the extra cooking. It was most important for Dad, however. Before the grain was cut, hail, a hard rain, or wind could ruin a crop. Aside from having his crop safe, Dad also looked forward to the crew's company and to hearing the local news some of them were sure to pass on.

Most of the farms in Pleasant Valley were too small for their owners to purchase their own threshing machines. The man who owned the threshing machine traveled from one farm to another, and Dad made a pretty good guess when they'd arrive by finding out how many farms they had to finish before getting to our place. Anxious to have our harvest done for the year, he would see that all the grain was cut and shocked before the arrival of the threshing equipment. Only two or three men traveled with the thresher, and getting the rest of the crew together was Dad's responsibility.

Dad and Lester worked on one of the four hay wagons, because it took that many wagons to keep the thresher busy. The threshing machine operator didn't want to shut it down while waiting for the next load, so the men couldn't waste any time. As soon as each wagon finished unloading, it headed back to the field for another load.

With much clanking and rattling of the gears, wheels, pipes, levers and other metal parts, the threshing machine performed its magic. It beat the grain heads off the stalks and loosened the hulls from around each kernel of grain, and shook them over a vibrating screen, where a fan blew away the chaff and straw. The heavy kernels of grain fell through the screen into the pipe, which funneled them down a two-ended grain spout to the waiting gunnysack. The straw and chaff blew out a bigger pipe, forming a straw stack. When the stack was as high as the spout, the man tending the pipe swung it over to one side and started making a new stack.

A lever directed the flow of grain as it rushed into a gunnysack that reached to the ground. The bagger gathered up the end of the sack with one hand and whipped a length of binding twine around in a "miller's" knot to keep the grain from spilling. One of the men helped Paul hoist the hundred-pound sacks into his grain wagon. When the wagon was full, Paul drove to the granary and emptied the sacks into the grain bins.

Leola, Effie and the twins were too young to do any fieldwork, and although Dora and I, at eleven and fourteen, helped shock grain, haul hay, haul rocks out of the fields on the stoneboat, and weed the rows of corn and potatoes, we didn't help with threshing. We didn't have the strength or stamina for pitching bundles all day. Besides that, Mom needed us in the kitchen. Preparing dinner and supper for the nine of us, plus the threshing crew of ten men, was a lot of work.Those hard-working men could put away a lot of food.

Although our meals were simple, they made up for it in quantity. There was always plenty of meat, potatoes and gravy, vegetables, beets and cucumber pickles, tomatoes, Jello salad, honey, bread, and butter, along with pitchers of Kool-Aid and pie for dessert. To make our Jello salad set up, since we didn't have a refrigerator or an icebox, we put the bowl in the creek, surrounded it with rocks so it wouldn't tip over, and kept it high enough so the water couldn't run into it. The cool water would set the Jello nicely.

Each morning we baked five or six different pies in the woodstove, which made our kitchen the hottest place in the house. The threshing crew's favorite was apple pie, but we also baked peach, cherry, huckleberry, coconut, lemon and our own special brand of "pumpkin" pies.

Since we couldn't grow pumpkins on our land, we used carrots from our garden. We boiled them, mashed them, and added the same spices we used for pumpkin pies. The substitution worked; the pies were good, and the men didn't care that the pies were made from carrots.

Most of our food came fresh from our garden and from our supply of canned goods in the cellar. We had a few apple, cherry and prune trees that yielded enough for canning to last the winter. To find huckleberries in late summer, we rode our horses clear up Monumental Mountain and picked the sweet, flavorful berries which we canned and used for pies.

The threshers liked Mom's fried chicken best, which she always managed to fix at least twice during their stay. But that meal took a lot more time to prepare — from catching the elusive birds, to killing, scalding, picking and singeing, to rinsing and cutting up. By the time she started frying the chicken pieces, we had already done a lot of work. It was a great deal easier to prepare ham and venison.

The crew arrived for dinner right at noon. After working around the threshing machine and pitching grain bundles all morning, the men were covered from head to toe with dust and chaff. Some of them asked us to sweep them off with a broom to get rid of the chaff, and washed their hands and faces outside in two granite washbowls, with towels, a bucket of water and a bar of soap placed alongside.

Mealtime was a happy occasion. The men joshed each other and told funny stories that had happened that day. Mom, Dora and

I kept busy refilling bowls and platters, enjoying the friendly bantering.

One meal I happened to be the butt of their jokes, and I ended up being embarrassed. I handed a jar of honey to Clarence Carson, an unmarried young man, asking, "Do you want some honey, Clarence?"

Ernie McKinney, who was always teasing me, laughingly revised my question to, "Do you want some, Honey Clarence?"

Being a little bashful, I was embarrassed that Ernie had made it sound like I called a man "Honey." Everyone at the table joined in the lighthearted laughter. Even Dad had a wide grin on his face. With my face glowing red, I whirled around, took the shortest way out of the room, flew through Mom's bedroom, and climbed out the open window. I stayed hidden until the men finished dinner and went back up the hill. My red face didn't last long. When the crew appeared again at suppertime, I was ready to do a little kidding myself.

⟨⟩   ⟨⟩

Effie recently reminded me about the "Honey Clarence" story which had so embarrassed me as a teenager. I've long since forgiven Ernie for his teasing and now remember how much fun that time had been for everyone — including me.

⟨⟩   ⟨⟩

Although the threshing crew worked hard and were hot, dirty and tired, they still made it an enjoyable experience. They razzed each other and played tricks on one another at every opportunity. There was a certain amount of planning and conniving going on to see who would be stuck with hauling the last load of bundles from the fields. The men would load their wagons either a little on the light side, or pile on a bigger load, whichever suited their needs to make their plan work. Sometimes a few men got together and decided that a certain wagon's crew would haul the last load. Then all day the connivers worked together to see if they could make the loads come out in such a way that the unsuspecting men would be the ones to make that last trip. When their plan worked, the plotters lounged around, resting, laughing and joking among themselves while the "victims" finished the last wagonload and took it to the thresher.

Our kitchen duties didn't keep Dora and me tied down all the time. When there was a little slack in the afternoon, we took Leola, Effie and the twins to the field to see the threshing machine. I liked watching the long belt go around and around, twisting and slapping as it ran from the tractor to the thresher. The whole outfit — tractor chugging away, long belt flapping and turning, threshing machine vibrating, rattling and shaking while gobbling up grain bundles and spitting out straw and grain — made a fascinating sight.

We enjoyed watching the grain bundles flying from pitchforks up to the top of the wagon, the men laughing as they worked, reins slapping, harnesses moving and creaking while the horses pulled hard on the loaded wagons. Everything was part of the excitement of threshing.

Despite the news, fun and good spirits the crew brought with them, it was fortunate for the cooks that threshing didn't take any longer than it did. Cooking large quantities for a big crew was a hard job and could turn into quite a problem. It was almost impossible to work the few leftovers into the next meal, and without ice or electricity, food wouldn't keep in the heat of the summer. Our only storage place was the cellar, which was merely cool, not cold. I could see why Mom heaved a sigh of relief when the threshers finished their work, drove their rigs out the gate and headed for the next farm.

But by the time the next harvest rolled around, we would have forgotten the hard work. We'd once again feel that inner excitement when the threshing crew drove through our gate, and started the whole process all over again.

42

Starting High School

On the first day of high school in September, 1938, Lester and I left the house early because we didn't want to miss the stub van that would pick us up at the junction. (Mom thought the name "stub van" was derived from the fact that it was a stubby little vehicle with no windows except in front.)

For the first time in our lives, we were no longer responsible for getting to school on our own. We would be riding buses to Kettle Falls, seventeen miles away. Thinking about riding in comfort gave me a twinge of guilt. Such luxury was a far cry from getting to school on horseback. Carrying notebooks, pencils, sack lunches, and the enrollment money in our pockets, we waited at the mailbox for the black stub van that would take us to Rice.

The driver, Walt Clemons, pulled to a stop beside us and opened the door for us. I found a spot beside Arlene Conner, who greeted me with a big smile. I guessed she was as excited about starting high school as I was. We stopped along the way to pick up all the other kids headed for school.

At Rice we transferred to a larger bus. I was surprised how long it was. Two back-to-back benches in the center divided the space into lengthwise sections, one for girls and the other for boys. Two benches with backs against the windows gave the bus four long seats that looked like they could hold forty kids. Obeying the driver's rules, I sat in the girls' section, while the boys sat on the far side.

About seven miles out of Rice, the highway sloped down a steep grade to the sandy flats along the Columbia River, where truck farms and orchards used to be. In preparation for the backwaters from Grand Coulee Dam, workers had begun clearing buildings and trees below a certain level. Seeing all this activity made me think of how green and fertile this irrigated area used to be. Llewelyn Gardens, a white painted wooden sign over its gate, had been one of the largest truck farms in this area. Their vegetables never looked puckered up for lack of water like some of our field plantings that never received water unless it rained.

I remember the summer I was five and our family had gone to Llewellyn Gardens to pick tomatoes for canning. Lester and I picked right alongside our parents, who didn't care if we ate a few ripe ones while we were filling our pails. I was hungry, and the first dead-ripe tomatoes tasted so good that I ate too many. On the way home, as the Star was rattling along at about thirty miles an hour, I needed to go to the toilet. But not seeing a good place to pull off the road and thinking I could wait until we got home, I didn't inform anyone of my dilemma. By the time we reached home, it was too late. — I had dirtied my bloomers. When Dad pulled up in front of our house and got out, he sniffed the air, looked at me, and asked why I hadn't told him I needed to stop.

"We were going too fast, and there was no place to stop," I wailed as Mom led me off to clean me up. Years later, I still felt the embarrassment of that moment.

After passing the truck farms, our bus crossed the Colville River on the iron-trussed bridge near where it flowed into the Columbia, and the shade trees and buildings of Kettle Falls came into sight. In no time at all we were going down Main Street and headed for the high school.

Other buses brought high school students from the other outlying areas of Kelly Hill, Highland, Greenwood and Meyers Falls. For the first time in our lives, Pleasant Valley students would have a lot of strangers for classmates.

Compared to our country grade school, where I had gone for eight years, the new school seemed huge. I felt lost in the large building, where we had different rooms for each class. On that first day, I didn't even know where to go when the bell rang. Rose Aubertin, a pretty Kettle Falls girl with shining black hair and a dazzling smile, offered to take me around.

During that day, whenever the bell rang, I followed Rose to the different classrooms. The first time I felt relaxed in my new surroundings was a few days later, when several of us country girls ate lunch together outside. Arlene Conner, Ellen McNutt, Effie Ball, Dorothea Heide, Hazel Rose and I sat on the lawn under the cool shade of the locusts, enjoying our break.

Being thrown in with strangers in new surroundings made me timid and shy, and uncomfortably aware of my buck teeth. My mirror had told me my teeth stuck out, but it hadn't bothered me because I'd always been in the midst of friends. But among strangers, I felt like an ugly duckling.

My new feeling of timidity puzzled me. I was still the same girl who had killed rattlesnakes and coyotes, fearlessly ridden the quaking aspen trees to the ground, and stuck like flypaper to the back of a horse while galloping across the fields and confidently jumping ditches. I wondered how many of these town kids — boys or girls — could find their way around the mountain like I could, drive a team of horses or shoot squirrels? Knowing my accomplishments and talents no longer counted, I felt cowed and less than I was.

Later in the fall, the sophomore students sponsored a welcome dance for our class at the grange hall not far out of Kettle Falls. Our advisor, Miss Gladys Graupner, told us we should contribute cookies or Kool-Aid to help with refreshments. That day while Lester and I were at school, Mom had made oatmeal cookies for us to take.

When we got to the hall and I started putting the cookies on plates, I found several had broken during the ride. The round cardboard oatmeal container hadn't protected them well enough. I put the broken pieces on the plate along with the perfect cookies, figuring they tasted just as good as the others. While Arlene, Rose and I were putting cookies on plates, one of the Kettle boys started helping himself. After sampling the broken cookies, he poked fun at them. "I wonder who would bring broken-up cookies like that," he said, while stuffing more pieces into his mouth. "You'd think they'd be too ashamed."

He didn't know they were my contribution, nor did he notice that his remarks made me too timid to claim them. Rose had seen me carrying the round box of cookies into the hall and got fed up with his disparaging comments. After his third complaint, she looked him straight in the eye and proclaimed, "If the cookies are so bad, maybe you shouldn't eat any more."

When the dance was over, I noticed all of Mom's cookies were gone — even the broken ones.

That winter, the freshman class hosted the sophomores at a sleigh-riding party on the Hays Hill — where we had our winter fun since I was a small girl — and I didn't feel out of place at all.

I knew high school would be exciting, but I hadn't realized I would witness the many changes the landscape would undergo. During my first year in high school, I became accustomed to the luxury of riding a bus. Guilt no longer rode with me for enjoying its ease or for depending on someone else to get me to school.

⋙ ⋘

Twenty-five years after feeling like an ugly duckling because of my buck teeth, I found Dr. Matthews, an orthodontist, who helped me feel more like a swan.

43

The Rising Waters

The backwater from Grand Coulee Dam would rise and cover hundreds of acres in our area — the highway from the bottom of the grade below Engleson's farm to Kettle Falls and beyond, the bridge over the Colville River, a nearby Indian burial ground, and the whole town of Kettle Falls. It would also cover and silence forever that thundering roar of the raging cascades of Kettle Falls. Remembering how its rushing torrents had held me spellbound as a child standing on the riverbank watching the Indians fish for salmon, I couldn't believe those falls would disappear.

Surveyors appeared along the river above the dam site, peering through their transits, measuring distances and leaving yellow-ribboned stakes behind. They pounded the stakes in the ground at 1,310 feet above sea level — the expected water line of the lake behind the dam. When we saw their yellow ribbons a mile or more from the river, we couldn't believe the Columbia would rise that much.

Workmen had almost completed construction of the dam, which began in 1933 and which would generate electricity and irrigate the desert land in the Columbia Basin. When the floodgates closed, the mighty river would rise and flood all the land: farms, homes, towns and much of State Highway 22. The lake behind the dam would be 151 miles long, backing clear up to the Canadian border.

All year long, from the school bus windows, we watched as drastic changes took place along the Columbia. A highway crew built a new road at a higher level, and house movers jacked up buildings and transported them to higher ground.

Loggers cut down timber and trees below the surveyors' stakes, loaded them onto trucks and hauled them off to a sawmill. On hastily constructed logging roads, the heavy trucks trailed dirty dust clouds behind as they plowed through the powdery soil. Great puffs of smoke floated in the sky from the burning fruit trees, pine and fir branches, including the beautiful fruit trees in the Llewelyn Gardens and other orchards along the river.

After the new highway was finished, which included a concrete bridge upstream across the Colville River, workers tore down the old iron and steel bridge. That site would soon be under water, since the Columbia would back up more than two miles into the mouth of the Colville River.

Since the rising water would cover the old Indian burial ground near the Colville River, the graves had to be located, and the remains dug up and moved to higher ground. As always, Dad, eager to earn extra money, took a job working on the crew that would dig up and rebury the bones. He had dug graves in the Mountain View Cemetery above Rice for friends who had died, but he had never dug up human remains. After his first day on the job, he came home sick to his stomach "By grab," he said, " digging up those bones just about made me pass out. We had to sort the bones, assemble a complete skeleton, and put it into each wooden box. Handling those human bones made me just as dizzy as seeing human blood."

The work wasn't as hard as some of the other jobs he taken on, but as far as he was concerned, it was the worst he ever had. But he was the family provider, and despite getting sick to his stomach every day, he stuck it out until the work was completed.

We watched as the state highway crews arrived with their dump trucks, bulldozers, and big equipment and began to build a new road. We could hear the racket of the road crew's machines through the open windows of the bus. Dump trucks hauled in ton after ton of huge boulders to fill in the low spot at the bottom of that first grade. Rocks clanged against the dump trucks' metal sides during loading and again when they were dumped. The bulldozers made more noise than the dump trucks. With powerful engines roaring, gears screeching, and blades clanging against boulders, they gouged out a new road, going up the high bank. As they advanced and backed up while digging and scraping, the ponderous machines clanked and belched smoke, and sent up more clouds of dust.

In the spring of 1939, workers started pouring into the area to move the town to its new location with their special equipment. They brought along their own houses to live in — little houses on wheels which they towed behind their cars or pickup.

They jacked up houses off their foundations and put them on huge flatbed trailers. Powerful trucks pulled them up the main street, stopping at each intersection so the men on the roofs could move overhead wires out of the way. At times, five houses in a row crept up the road and out of town. The trucks slowed to a crawl as they climbed the winding grade leading toward the town of Meyers Falls.

When the school year ended in May of 1939, workers dismantled the high school and moved it a section at a time. That fall, sophomores, juniors and seniors went to the same red brick building they attended the previous year, but in a different location.

The people in the towns of Kettle Falls and Meyers Falls had an ongoing argument over the name of the combined town. Since the site had been named Meyers Falls for many years, its residents wanted to retain the name. But the Kettle Falls people, whose businesses, telephone office and post office had moved, wanted the town's name changed to Kettle Falls. Finally, federal officials settled the argument. Since Meyers Falls had never had a post office, they declared the town had to be named Kettle Falls. To differentiate between the two, we called the combined town New Kettle, and the previous site Old Kettle.

Coulee Dam's floodgates were closed in late 1940, and the river started backing up. It overflowed its banks and kept rising. The next summer, when the backwater neared the falls at Kettle, Indians began arriving, some coming from miles away, as they had when they fished for salmon. They gathered to hold a Ceremony of Tears, as they watched the water inching up the falls, finally covering them. Centuries of salmon fishing at the falls was over forever.

⟐ ⟐

It wasn't the backwater that ended their fishing, or the absence of the falls, but the fact that the salmon had no way of getting past Coulee Dam on their way from the ocean to their spawning grounds. The prohibitive cost of building fish ladders around the 550-foot dam kept engineers from drawing plans for them.

⟐ ⟐

We had witnessed the uprooting of a whole town. Cement foundations littered the site and were all that was left of Old Kettle. Houses had been moved, except for those few located safely above the high-water line. The following fall, when we went to high school at New Kettle, our bus traveled the highway we had watched being built. When spring arrived, we saw the water rise higher and higher, creeping up over the flats where we had picked tomatoes and where all the gardens had been, until the river finally covered the old highway. Seeing the black pavement leading straight out into the Columbia gave me an eerie feeling. I was glad the bus wasn't taking that road any longer, as the river continued rising. By the summer of 1941, the Columbia River reached the yellow-ribboned stakes.

The new highway presented us with different scenery, as it followed the wide expanse of the shining lake to the mouth of the Colville River, where the rising waters had formed a beautiful cove. The river narrowed at the new concrete bridge, which had no high railings or supports to obstruct the view. Past the bridge, a long, sandy grade studded with pine trees led to the top of a ridge, from where we caught a glimpse of the Colville River tumbling off the hill into the cascade called Meyers Falls. Soon we arrived in the new town of Kettle Falls, where most of the houses from the old site had been relocated.

After the river climbed its banks, it changed from a fierce turbulence with a strong current to a quiet stretch, gliding smoothly along with no sign of a current, without rapids or falls. The river had spread and was almost three miles wide along the flats near where Rickey Canyon Road junctioned with the highway. And further upriver, at Marcus Flats, it spread out to four miles wide.

The bright sun made the huge lake almost bluer than the sky. I wished we had a boat so we could explore places we hadn't seen. But I never had any desire to go upstream over the spot where the falls used to be. Remembering those thundering cataracts, I could imagine the churning water under the surface and thought there would be turbulence and whirlpools. Before the Coulee Dam was built — when the Columbia was dangerous with its strong current and its eddies and whirlpools — I hadn't wanted to cross it on the ferry, much less be out on it in a small boat. But now it was different; the dam had tamed the upper part of the Columbia.

⟨⟩ ⟨⟩

The December 1971 issue of *Reader's Digest* describes the dam: "…Seventy-five miles west of Spokane is an awesome sight: Grand Coulee Dam, which stands athwart the Columbia River like a fortress, the water foaming over it; spillway forming a rainbow waterfall twice as high as Niagara Falls. The dam is more than twelve city blocks across; the water it backs up forms Franklin D. Roosevelt Lake, which stretches to Canada — 151 miles…."

A national recreation site now encompasses the part of Old Kettle not covered by water, some of which is the spot where the high school once stood. In 1967, my classmates, Rose Aubertin Geer, Bernice Lewis Bailey and Ralph Byrd arranged to have our twenty-fifth reunion picnic there. The continuing every-other-year reunions have turned into an "Old Kettle Reunion." After all these years — after the town moved and after the river rose, we're still eating our lunch in the shade of the tall locust trees where the high school once stood.

In August 1989, area people celebrated the fiftieth year since the town of Kettle Falls moved. Louis and Jo Nullett put together a large pictorial display showing the "old days." Contributors dug out pictures from their albums and made them a part of the display. There were pictures of buildings being hauled away, of Indians fishing, of the falls that gave the town its name, and pictures of pioneers. This display is now in the Kettle Falls Public Library.

My Christmas Card Route

One day I read in a magazine that one could earn money by selling Christmas cards. The cards came in a box of fifty, and the advertisement suggested to sell the cards at a dime each. I placed my order, and when the cards arrived, I was ready to go.

Selling Christmas cards seemed like a good idea. It was the only way I knew a fourteen-year-old girl living in the eastern Washington countryside could earn money in the winter of 1938. Dad couldn't give us spending money; what with such a big family, we barely had enough for necessities. I'd heard a lot of talk about the Depression and guessed it meant everyone else was strapped for money, too.

I bridled Betty and set off to sell cards to our neighbors. Head down, Betty plodded up the steep Folsom Hill, her nostrils blowing twin columns of steam into the cold November air.

Riding bareback, I felt the sorrel mare's body heat through my overalls, keeping me warm. For once, I was glad we didn't own a saddle.

Although we hadn't had snow at our level yet, it had powdered the trees on top of the mountain. Mom had laid down the law to wear our long wool underwear, which were awfully scratchy but kept us from freezing. I had also put on a warm, long-sleeved flannel shirt, my sturdy bib overalls, a sweater, a heavy jacket, my stocking cap and gloves. I dropped the box of cards into my old denim lunch bag from the days I had ridden a horse to school.

My first stop was Paul and Ethel Holter's. I spread my wares out on the kitchen table, and Ethel selected four and gave me forty cents. Putting the coins in my pocket, I thanked her and left, happy with my first sale. Five minutes later, I rode in to Ella Loven's yard, tied Betty to a fencepost, and walked to the kitchen door. Surprised, Ella greeted me, "Well, Ines, come in, come in. What are you doing out on a cold day like this?"

I handed her the box of Christmas cards and told her I was earning money by selling them. Soon I was on my way again with more coins in my pocket and fewer cards in the box. Betty plodded uphill to my next stop, our good neighbors the Mathises. I remembered the winter I was in first grade and didn't have any mittens. Mrs. Mathis had sewn several pairs of mittens from wool material and sent them to school. At recess, Miss Dean passed out the mittens and handed me a pair. I was surprised and grateful — I never had cold hands again. Eight years later, Mrs. Mathis was just as kind by buying some Christmas cards from me.

On I went to John and Dessie Byrd's farm. Dessie was surprised to see me, since I didn't make it a habit of visiting neighbors past Folsom Hill. Dessie picked out some cards, and I added more money to my pocket. Climbing on Betty again, I rode down the steep pitch to the Ebbie Conner house. While Gladys picked out a couple of cards, I enjoyed the warmth of the stove and was soon headed to Giberson's, a short ride downhill.

I rode against a blustery wind, which went right through my several layers of winter clothes. Shivering from the cold, I wished I was done and could go home. Getting to Giberson's, I slid off Betty and tied her up. As Wilma opened the door and I stepped in, the heat from the wood stove hit me in the face. I was glad to be out of the icy wind for a while. In the fifteen minutes it took for them to look at the cards, I warmed up again. Deciding which to buy, they admired them all, exclaiming over the pretty pictures.

I hated to leave the cozy, warm house but went out again and climbed on Betty. The bitter, cold wind tore at my face, stinging my cheeks and turning my nose numb. My fingers in their thin gloves soon felt like brittle sticks, and I wished for wool mittens like those Mrs. Mathis had given me in the first grade.

Because of the miserable, blustery cold, I decided to make only one more stop at the Lonnie Conners', and then go on home. I looked forward to seeing Arlene, who was a lot of fun. She had no sisters and was always glad to see me. While Nina looked at my dwindling supply of cards, Arlene and I had fun talking.

After my pleasant visit, I got on Betty again and rode through the cleft in the hills on the narrow road that came out at the Pleasant Valley School. The tall trees acted as a barrier against the wind, which made it not nearly as cold, and I decided to make two more calls.

I figured the McCarrolls probably needed at least one card, too. After brief stops there and at the Heideggers', I struck out for home. Somehow, Betty knew she was heading for the barn; she raised her head against the wind and increased her pace.

By the time I finished the five-mile loop, I had stopped at most of the houses along the way. No one had much money to spare for such luxuries as Christmas cards, but almost everyone had bought at least one card — some as many as five. I had a feeling they probably felt sorry for me riding around on such a cold and windy day.

I was excited when I told Mom that I sold most of the cards, as I poured the coins on the table. They clattered and clinked as they made a loose pile of silver. "Just look at all the money, Mom! I sold all but five cards."

Mom looked at the money — and at the few remaining cards — and said, "That's good! I'll use those to send to Grandma and your uncles and aunts."

She sent a check to the greeting card company for the cost of the cards, and I got to keep the profit. I had earned a little over a dollar — big money — on my Christmas card route.

45

Visit in Idaho

One morning Uncle Bob pulled his car to a stop in our front yard, opened the door, and swung his white-shod feet to the ground. White shoes on a man! Astonishing! Farm men always wore brown or black ones. Only women and girls wore white shoes. But I had to admit they made Bob look spiffy; all dressed up.

Since the Depression — bad times for all —kept our families from visiting one another, it was always a welcome surprise when a family member dropped in on us. Knowing Bob had to scrimp to get a few dollars together for the trip made us appreciate his visit.

He stayed for just a day, and before he was ready to leave, he asked Mom if I could go back to Lewiston with him for a couple of weeks. "She'd be good company on the long drive home, and I want her to meet Agnes and the boys, and her other cousins."

"I guess I could do without her right now, and it would be good for her to be with some of her relatives again," Mom said.

I had overheard the conversation and could hardly contain my excitement until Mom asked if I'd like to go. My answer was out before she finished. "Yes, I sure would. I'd like to see all our relatives !"

I got out Mom's small black suitcase, the only one we had, and hurriedly put in a couple pair of overalls and shirts, a dress and some underclothes. I was ready to go. Mom had to remind me to take along a comb and my toothbrush.

Bob explained the route, which would take us through Spokane and then south to Lewiston. Since I'd rarely been as far away as the hundred miles to Spokane, and had never been to Lewiston, I didn't care what highway he drove. It was all new and interesting to me.

Suddenly, as we were driving on a straight stretch of road, Bob asked, "How would you like to take the wheel?"

That really startled me. I'd always thought it would be fun to drive. So before Bob could change his mind, I quickly said, "Heck, yes. I don't know how to drive, but I'd like to try."

Although I was fifteen, neither Lester nor I had been given the opportunity to drive. One night after a dance, Lester took it upon himself to get the Nash started, and ended up stalling in the middle of the road. Dad was angry and punished him by making him walk home alone from the grange hall.

Bob stopped the car on the side of the road, and we changed places. I was so excited my hands were shaking as I gripped the big steering wheel. "What do I do first?" I asked.

Bob pointed to the starter and the clutch and explained how they worked. Dutifully, I followed instructions. I started the engine while Bob instructed me on the function and operation of the gear shift and clutch. It wasn't complicated at all and only a matter of timing. It was easy to keep the car going straight and on the right side of the road. I thought we were going pretty fast, but I was too busy watching the road to look at the the speedometer. I was glad when Bob said, "You're going about fifty miles an hour; you'd better ease up on the gas." I slowed down to a safer speed for a first-time driver.

As we approached the Spokane River, I took a good look at the bridge, and thought it to be pretty narrow. Luckily, no other cars were approaching from the opposite direction, and I could stay almost in the middle of the bridge. Once across, I decided I'd had enough driving for one day; I was getting a little nervous. Bob told me how to bring the car safely to a stop, and I felt my first attempt at driving was a success.

At Bob's house, a dark-haired woman in a bright green satin blouse, Aunt Agnes, greeted me. Though surprised at the unexpected company, she made me feel welcome. Only seven years older than I, she seemed more like an older sister than an aunt. Agnes showed me "my" room. It was hard to imagine having a whole room all to myself after having shared an attic bedroom with a brother and five sisters.

Agnes' father, "Grandpa" Nelson, soon came home from his walk with his two small grandsons, Bobby and Arden. Later in the evening, another cousin, Lorene "Tacky" Hunt, came to spend the night. She had visited us once on the farm with Aunt Lizzie and her boys. Since Tacky's mother was dead and her father frequently worked away from home, she lived with Uncle Lester and Aunt Lizzie part of the time.

Tacky was younger than I by a couple of years, but she knew a lot more about living in a city. At bedtime, I started peeling off my clothes, and Tacky gasped when she saw the window shades still up and me half-undressed. She said, "You're supposed to pull the shades before you undress!" and ran to pull them down.

At home on the farm, we didn't have shades to pull, or curtains to close. When anyone came near the house, the dogs barked, and we knew someone was approaching. In the city, a sidewalk ran in front of the houses and pushed in on each side, and there was no dog to warn that someone was near.

To my delight, Bob soon gave me my second driving lesson. He must have been a good teacher, because I felt quite confident, managed to shift gears by myself, and I only killed the engine once when I forgot to step on the clutch as I came to a stop.

During my visit I asked Bob if he'd take me to see my cousins at Uncle Lester's house. He looked at me, pulled his keys out of his pocket and handed them to me, saying, "Take the car and go see them."

I wasn't so sure I could drive clear across town on my own, but Bob reassured me by saying, "You know the way, so you should be able to get there by yourself." What confidence!

I got into the car, stepped on the clutch, turned the key, stomped on the starter, put the gear shift into low, and started off. I was going through town feeling pretty good until I suddenly remembered the narrow Eighteenth Street Bridge across the Clearwater River. When I got to the bridge, traffic was brisk and several cars were coming at me from the opposite direction. But despite my worries, by driving cautiously, staying out of the path of other cars, I made it all the way across without hitting any cars or the bridge.

My cousins didn't have any chores for that afternoon while their parents were at work. The day was too warm for outdoor games to interest us, so we stayed inside, spending the time with idle talk. Noticing Aunt Lizzie's ironing basket full of clothes, I told Guy I'd iron them. He plugged in the electric iron, which was faster on shirts and dresses than our old flatirons at home that had to be heated on the stove. I went through that whole basket of clothes while we were talking and arguing.

While it was still daylight, I left to return to Bob's house and was looking forward to another go at driving. It was exciting! Crossing the bridge didn't make me nervous anymore, but realizing later I had been driving without a license made me shiver. I was just grateful I hadn't run into anything.

My two-week visit passed in a flash, and it was time to return to Pleasant Valley. I'd been homesick on a couple of occasions, even though I had a wonderful time. As I put my few clothes back into the suitcase, I looked around the big bedroom that had been all mine. Bob and Agnes drove me to the bus depot, where we said our goodbyes.

When my bus pulled into the station at Colville, Mom, Dad, and my sisters were waiting for me. I was so glad to see them; I hadn't realized I'd missed them so much.

The next day, as I was hoeing weeds at the Garner Place with Mom, Dora, Leola and Effie, I looked at the beauty of the timbered hills and mountains around us and realized how lovely it was compared to the city I had just left. While I had enjoyed my visit, I came to the decision that life in the city would be boring, what without chores or outdoor activities. I understood why Bob hadn't wanted to wear his white shoes to help Dad with the barn chores.

⟨⟩   ⟨⟩

Thirty years later I again visited the area and discovered that a new highway had bypassed Lewiston Hill. Uncle Bob gave me a copy of his poem that had been published, entitled, "That Lewiston Hill."

46

Deer Hunting

Deer hunting was not much of a sport for us, but it was almost the only means by which we could put meat on the table — except for the chickens we raised. It wasn't a simple matter to feed our family of eight. But everyone else was in the same boat —hunting deer for the table was a way of life. Dad was a good hunter and he enjoyed being out in the wilds, and for every hunt there was a story to tell.

We often heard about the time when one of Dad's hunting partners, Bill Preston, was straddling the limp form of the buck lying on the ground, grabbing an antler with one hand, his hunting knife in the other, ready to cut the deer's throat. But before he could make his slash, the deer sprang to its feet, flinging the surprised hunter up onto its back, who was too startled to do anything but hang on.

Dad and Pearl Entwistle came into the clearing just in time to see the wounded deer tearing downhill with Bill clinging to its back. Hanging onto an antler, he had his long legs wrapped around the animal's belly. After crashing through brush and jumping across deadfalls, Bill was finally able to reach forward and cut the deer's throat and end his ride.

When Dad and Pearl caught up with him, they asked why he had stayed on the deer. Bill replied, "We were all out of meat, so I couldn't let it get away." After a pause, he added, "It was about time I killed it; I couldn't have hung on much longer!"

The two men razzed Bill Preston for years about his wild ride, but he enjoyed the telling of it as much as anyone. It remained one of their best deer-hunting stories.

Dad was the best hunter in Pleasant Valley; Bill Preston and Pearl were the best in the Arzina area. These men were excellent shots. Having spent a lot of time hunting to keep meat on the table, they knew where the deer were most likely to be found, where they laid up while resting, and when they might be moving about.

Bill Preston lived by himself in a small cabin on land that didn't produce much in the way of income. Most of his property was timbered, but he didn't have it logged off because the sawmills' price for logs had fallen. He derived his main source of income from a small herd of sheep, which he raised with the help of his big black and white dog, Bouncie. Bill had come from the hills of Tennessee and still spoke in a soft Southern drawl. We loved to hear him talk. He always pronounced Pearl's name as "Pearlie," which we thought sounded funny.

Mom and Goldie often hunted with the three men, as did Lester, Dora and I on weekends. We girls acted as drivers, while Lester carried a rifle and often took a stand. Mom left Leola to take charge of the house while the rest of us were gone. At eight, Leola was very responsible, and Mom could depend on her to feed Effie and the twins, and keep them safe and out of trouble.

When we hunted nearby on Monumental Mountain, we walked up the ridges that fanned out from our house. We had to start out early because Dad wanted to be on a stand by daylight, before the deer started moving about. He woke us up at four in the morning by yelling his old logging-camp wake-up call, "Daylight in the swamp!"

While Mom made breakfast by the light of the kerosene lamp, I fixed sandwiches. We wrapped them in wax paper and slid them inside our shirts, where they stayed snug against our backs if we kept our shirttails tucked in. We needed our hands free for carrying guns and grabbing branches to pull ourselves up the steepest slopes.

When we hunted close to the top of the mountain, Dad drove us part way so we didn't have to walk so far. It was also good to have the truck as close as possible to the spot we hunted for ease in carrying out the game. It took two strong men to haul a deer, while we girls carried the heart and the liver.

Although there weren't any signposts on the mountain, we knew which section Dad was describing when he told us where we were going to hunt. Unless an area was already named — like Carter Canyon, Maggie Folsom's Cabin or John Marty's Mine, the hunters picked names for different areas. Goldie Entwistle had a favorite spot for a stand, so we all got to calling it "Goldie's Stand." Everyone knew Dad's favorite place and called it "Bill's Stand." Then there was Tamarack Thicket, Flat Rock, Salt Lick and Rock Canyon.

Dad told us where to start and end our drives, and his instructions went something like: "We'll be on our stands by daylight. You kids start your drive about a half-hour after that below the thicket at the bottom of the canyon. When you finish your drive, meet us up the hill from Flat Rock."

The features of the hills and mountains became our signposts. Dad had started our hunting lessons when we lived on the Curry Place, and we had become accustomed to noting the characteristics of terrain — tree growth, rock bluffs, game trails, and other distinctive features when going through the woods. There were plenty of familiar landmarks, and no one ever got lost on one of Dad's hunts.

During almost every hunting season, men from Spokane or Seattle came to hunt with us. Some were relatives or friends of the regular hunting party, but often total strangers appeared, hoping to hunt with us. Dad never turned them away, and he invited them to join us under one condition: "No liquor while hunting." He felt strongly that anyone carrying a gun should not be carrying a bottle.

Most of the city hunters carried high-powered rifles with telescope sights, and sported big hunting knives strapped to their belts. Some even had field glasses strung around their necks. Their special equipment and hunting clothes — visored red caps and red plaid jackets with big pockets — seemed overdone compared to Dad's simple dress and equipment. His hunting clothes were his everyday garb — a cotton flannel shirt, bib overalls, denim jacket, and a beat-up gray felt hat. His total equipment consisted of a rifle with open sights, a jackknife, a thin round whetstone, and a short length of rope. Bill Preston and Pearl were similarly dressed and equipped.

All the latest equipment and fancy clothes didn't make the outsiders better hunters or guarantee them a deer. Some of the city hunters were after the biggest buck they could find. It's no wonder their wives refused to eat the meat they brought home. A buck with a big rack of antlers with many points was almost certain to be an old one and its meat was bound to be tough. In the rutting season during late fall, the bucks' necks swelled in preparation for the fights they'd have over the does. If a hunter killed this trophy buck at that time, parts of the meat were strong and not fit to eat. Dad was more interested in getting a deer that was good eating than in getting one with a big rack. All he did with the antlers was toss them over the top of the barbed-wire fence around our yard or nail them against one side of the granary.

The most memorable hunt Dad ever organized resulted in seven bucks being killed on the same day. I missed all the excitement, because by that time I had left home. But hearing all about it, I pieced together the event.

Louie Koerner, Ralph Lawson and his daughter, Darlene, joined Mom, Dad, Lester and Dora in the hills near the Lawson place. Early in the morning, several does and bucks ran past Dad and Louie on their separate stands. Each had a clear shot and brought down a buck. As the remaining deer topped the rise, Mom fired away, getting another one.

Pleased with their success, the hunting party left the stand. Dad had his strategy all worked out for what was to come next. "Since Louie, Sis and I got our bucks, we'll make the next drive. Maybe you can hit some of those bucks we're gonna chase past you!" With that he pointed to where he wanted his friends to take their stands.

Not wanting to spook the deer, Dad, Mom and Louie waited for a good hour before quietly working their way down toward the bottom of the next canyon. As they turned and headed uphill, they made a lot of a lot of noise, hoping to scare deer toward the four on stands. About fifteen minutes later, they heard the boom of two rifles, followed by the sound of more shots, which echoed back and forth between the ridges. When the firing stopped and the mountain was quiet again, the threesome continued uphill and reached Lester, who proudly pointed to the big buck he had shot. The other three hunters couldn't get over how easy it had been to bag three bucks of their own.

The sound of shots echoing through the canyon probably made it the noisiest deer hunt anybody ever heard. It was also the most successful hunt our group ever experienced — each hunter got a buck. A picture of the hunters and their bucks eventually appeared in the *Statesman-Index*, Colville's weekly newspaper.

The local farmers all butchered their own meat. While the weather was still warm, Mom set aside enough meat to last us for two or three days. She canned the meat in jars or put some of it raw in half-gallon fruit jars and kept it cool in the creek. The water was so cold that the meat kept fresh for as long as three weeks.

After quartering the deer, Dad wrapped each quarter in a white cloth to keep the flies off, then hung it from braces on the woodshed. The longer the meat could hang, the more tender and flavorful it became, and that could only be done if the weather was cold. We were glad when Dad got a deer after cold weather set in — that's when Mom made jerky.

Dad cut roasts for suppers, but we enjoyed thin steaks best of all. Every morning Mom lugged a quarter side into the kitchen and sliced off steaks to fry for breakfast. Most of us invented an excuse to go by the kitchen stove so we could sneak a piece of juicy meat off the platter, claiming we couldn't wait until breakfast. Mom sure knew how to cook venison.

Even though Dad enjoyed every hunting trip, we knew he most enjoyed hunting with the same group of friends. When the men got together after a hunt, they relived the excitement of each trip and had much fun recalling the events of the day, especially around the poker table. When Dad got together with his friends for a friendly game of penny-ante poker, the evening became an extension of their hunting trips.

When the men played at our house, the game continued long after we went to bed in our attic room. We listened to the sounds from below and could tell when the storyteller reached the exciting parts by the laughter booming up through the ceiling. We identified the players by the sound of their voices and the ring of their laughter. Dad's familiar deep laugh gave him away immediately, Louie's tended to be dry and choppy, while Ernie's lasted longer, and he laughed more often. Toar Lickfold's rich and vibrant chuckle turned into a rolling laugh that made everyone within earshot join in.

As Dora and I lay in bed sorting out their voices and listening to their laughter, we couldn't help laughing ourselves. We knew the men were off on one of their hunting trips, enjoying their experiences all over again. It never surprised us to hear Dad say, "You should — Bill Preston ride — buck — through — brush," ending with, "I couldn't have hung on — longer!" and hear the bursts of laughter. We didn't need to hear all the words. We knew that story by heart.

❧ ❧

Pearl's son, Billie, inherited a rifle Dad sold to his father. I'm hoping he will sell it to me someday, so I'll have something tangible that belonged to our hunting trips.

The photo of the seven deer hanging from the truck rack proves this hunt was successful. People have told me that Mom could fry the best venison steak in Pleasant Valley. The only steak that's come close to it in flavor and tenderness was the succulent Kobe beef I ate forty years later in a Japanese restaurant, renowned in all of Tokyo for its choice beef. Henry and I were visiting his son, Dick, and his wife, Jeaninne, who lived in Japan. When Irikin-san, the owner and a personal friend of Dick's, came to our table carrying a white-wrapped, aged quarter of beef to show us, my mind flew back over the years, and I saw Mom carrying a hindquarter of venison into our kitchen.

47

Lester Leaves Home

During our sophomore year in 1939, Lester quit school to look for a job. A friend of his, Rhodie Hunter, had heard that Potlach Lumber Company, in northern Idaho, was hiring a crew. It didn't take long for Lester to make up his mind. He wanted a job to earn some spending money. At seventeen, he was two years older than most kids in our class because he hadn't started school until he was seven years old, and had fallen behind in the fourth grade. He liked sports, but he didn't like studying or turning in assignments. In addition, he and Dad were having a few clashes. Lester was ready for a change.

Dad had always been strict with us three older kids, but he was hardest on Lester. He expected him to do a man's work, yet never praised him for anything and couldn't pay him — except on one rare occasion. He demanded instant obedience and didn't tolerate any backtalk. We never asked why; we all just did as we were told.

There was always work to do. All summer long Lester, Dora and I hoed weeds out of the four vegetable gardens besides doing our daily chores and helping with the grain harvest. Lester helped Dad milk and feed the cows, feed the pigs, clean out the barn, and harness the horses for the day's work. While Dad drove a team of two horses, Lester was likely to be driving another team, pulling a harrow or springtooth in another field.

One spring after plowing a field he was going to plant to grain, Dad surprised us by offering us a dollar apiece to haul rocks out of that field. He told us to use the stoneboat because it would be easier than the big wagon.

Lester harnessed a horse, hitched it to the stoneboat, and headed toward the field while Dora and I walked behind him. Tossing rocks on the stoneboat all day, we wondered what had brought about Dad's unexpected offer, since we had worked a lot harder at other jobs without being paid. We never did find out why this job was different.

When we complained to Mom about never getting any praise from Dad, she replied, "Dad doesn't brag on you because he doesn't want to give you a big head. He's proud of you, even though he doesn't tell you so."

When Rhodie appeared and announced he was looking for a job, Lester was ready. He was not happy with the amount of work he had to do for so little return in terms of appreciation or spending money. When he told Dad he was going with Rhodie, Dad told him he should stay home until he got out of school. But Lester stuck to his guns. It was the first time any of us had defied Dad.

Mom sided with Dad and added that Lester was too young to be on his own. Despite all arguments, Lester threw some belong-ings onto the back seat, climbed into his friend's car, and we watched in shocked silence as the car drove out of our gate.

That was the beginning of major change in our family. Mom worried about Lester every day. Her face had a closed, pinched expression, and her eyes wouldn't look at any of us. She didn't talk to Dad, silently blaming him for making it so tough on Lester that he left home. Dora and I weren't happy about our leader leaving, either, and hoped he would come back. He had led us in wild adventures as well as in our work. Without him, the adventures would stop, but the workload would increase.

When his job ended, Lester did come back. Mom's face lit up with smiles again, and her worried look never returned, even after Lester left to go on to his next job. He came to see us as often as his work allowed, especially in the fall during hunting season. But Lester couldn't come home to stay; he was making his own way.

⋖⋗ ⋖⋗

In 1989, Janice Entwistle Harlick and her husband, Joe, visited us in Tennessee. I asked Janice if she knew Dad had made us kids mad by bragging about how she had shocked hay because he never bragged on us — and we shocked hay every year. She said, "Yes," and we laughed together and talked about past activities in Pleasant Valley and Arzina.

48

Basil, the Hungry Hobo

Basil was a wandering man, and one day he wandered into our lives, asking if he could chop wood in exchange for a meal. We thought we were having a hard time during the Depression until hobos appeared on foot, looking for a meal or a place to work for board and room. Those who came to our door must have been desperately hungry to have found their way to our farm, six miles off the state highway. When they told their sad tales, we realized we weren't in such bad shape after all. Unlike them, we never went hungry and had a roof over our heads. Their first question was always, "Can I chop wood for a meal?"

Basil, it turned out, was something of a cook. He arrived one late afternoon, after Dad had finished his field work for the day. When Basil asked if he could chop wood for a meal, or work for board and room, he looked worried, almost scared. Dad gave him the same answer he gave all the other men: "I need some help, but I can't afford to hire anyone. But you can eat with us, and chop some wood if you like."

At breakfast, Basil put away three eggs, a mound of crispy fried potatoes, and three thick slices of homemade bread. His comment was simple: "Everything sure tastes good!"

These wandering men weren't beggars. They were merely hungry and on the move looking for work. If they were lucky, they found a farmer who could give them room and board in exchange for work. They hoped to get a meal and a place to spend the night if nothing more. Their offer to chop wood saved their pride and showed they were willing to work.

At mealtime Basil took three big helpings, apologizing to Mom for being so hungry. She smilingly replied, "That's all right. You can eat all you want." Eating as if he didn't know where his next meal was coming from, Basil said he hadn't had many square meals in the past year. Gaunt and strained, he looked like he had no money for food or anything else, and had gone hungry many times. His overalls, shirt and light jacket were frayed, almost worn out. He carried his only belongings in a paper bag, which couldn't have held more than an extra shirt, pants and socks.

At bedtime, Dad handed him a blanket and said, "You can sleep in the hay mow of the barn. But don't smoke or light any matches. I don't want my barn burned down."

The next morning, while Basil was helping Dad milk the cows, he asked if he could spend another night with us before moving on. Replying that it would be all right, Dad added, "Resting up an extra day would probably do you some good."

When the men came into the kitchen, Mom was mixing flour and potato water to start a batch of light bread. Saying he used to help his mother bake bread, Basil asked if he could help her form the rolls and loaves. A startled look came over Mom's face, but she smiled and said she'd like that. Not many men wanted to help make bread. Her brother, Bob, was the only other man who had ever volunteered his talents in the kitchen before.

Soon the two of them were happily pinching off dough and rolling it around to make smooth, round rolls. A big smile had replaced Basil's worried look, and he appeared to be a different man. After making bread and cinnamon rolls, Basil lent a hand preparing supper.

Our plentiful supper of potatoes, gravy, venison roast, vegetables and fresh-baked bread hit the spot. The delicious cinnamon rolls topped off the feast and filled us up. I felt sorry for our latest hobo guest. He might never get another chance to help make bread, and he faced many uncertain tomorrows with perhaps no bread at all.

After spending one more night in the hay mow and putting away another big breakfast, Basil got ready to leave. Picking up his pitiful bag of possessions, he thanked my parents for the good meals and a place to stay. Dad shook hands warmly and said regretfully, "You're a good worker, Basil. I wish I could take you on at board and room."

Mom handed Basil a cinnamon roll and two sandwiches and sent him on his way with her good wishes. Maybe Mom's generosity would keep him from starving until he found his next meal and a roof over his head.

My sisters and I stood in the yard, sadly watching him walk out through the gate and out of our lives. We hoped Basil would find a farmer who could afford a hired hand.

49

Chicken for Supper

"Go pick out a good-sized chicken and get it ready to fry," Mom told me. "We'll have chicken for supper tonight."

Getting a chicken ready to cook wasn't as simple as it sounded. Mom didn't mean for me to go to the Rice store and buy a chicken all cut up, ready for the skillet. She wanted me to catch one of our chickens running loose in the barnyard, chop its head off (which I had never done), pluck it, and cut it into pieces.

At sixteen, I'd had enough experience to know which one to choose. I didn't want a spring chicken that hadn't filled out yet, nor did I want one of the laying hens or a tough old rooster. I was going to pick a full-grown Rhode Island Red. I put a bucket of water on the cookstove so it would be hot for scalding the chicken later, and went looking for that "good-sized" fryer.

The chickens were near the granary and were scratching around for something to eat. Spotting one that was perfect, I began sneaking up on them before they could scatter in all directions. Getting close, I made a flying leap at the chosen one. Unfortunately, it dodged a split second after I leaped, and I came up with a handful of dirt instead of a feathered body. The chickens ran, squawking as they fluttered away. Keeping an eye on my target in the midst of the flock, I followed it around the granary and slowly edged up to it. This time I lunged before the chicken could dodge, and I grabbed it with both hands.

Holding the bird close to me, I headed for the chopping block in the woodshed. I dreaded having to cut off its head but I had seen it done. After all, I reasoned to myself, it couldn't be much different than chopping a piece of wood. I placed the chicken on the chopping block. On my first try, the chicken jerked its head aside and I chopped off its beak. On the next swing, I was fast and got the job done.

I dropped the headless body onto the clean wood chips by the chopping block to let it bleed out while it jumped around. I discovered that chopping its head off was harder than cutting a piece of wood. I swore to never again kill a chicken that way.

Still muttering to myself, I went into the house, picked up the bucket with the hot water, carried it outside, and plunged the chicken in the steaming water several times until the feathers came out easily. Next, I singed its white body to remove the fine feathers by rolling a newspaper into a torch and lighting it from the open fire in the stove. Holding the chicken over the stove, I ran the burning torch across one side, flipped it over, and singed the other side. The torch was getting short, so I tossed it quickly into the stove before I burnt my fingers. Once I hadn't been fast enough and had singed the hairs on my wrist.

I washed the chicken under the water faucet and began cutting it up with our sharpest butcher knife. I cleaned out its insides and cut the fryer into portions, rinsed the pieces once more, and left them draining in the colander. My job of getting a chicken ready for frying was finished. Mom had taught me every step.

The next time Mom asked me to get her a fryer for supper, I picked up the .22 and headed outside. I selected a good-sized chicken, took aim and fired. It was a very lucky shot: I hit my target in the head. When I took it to the chopping block, I chopped off its head in one smooth swing of the axe, I was glad to have found a way to get around the hardest part of getting a chicken ready for supper.

50

Mattress Making
at the Grange

It was during during the grange meeting that Dessie McCarroll, master of Quillisascut Grange, announced we could have new mattresses at little or no cost to us, as long as we were willing to work hard. The County Extension Agent, Mr. Millay, had told her that the Roosevelt Administration had a new program of furnishing raw materials to groups who would sponsor a mattress-making project. (Getting something without spending much money was important in 1941 — a time when no one had a penny to spare.)

Dessie explained that this project would help the families in Pleasant Valley, Arzina and Rice, at the same time using up government surplus cotton. Mr. Millay had explained there would be a training period for representatives. In addition to receiving training, those attending would receive written instructions on how to teach others to make mattresses. The event would take place at the grange hall, where there was enough room to set up big work tables.

I was glad for the opportunity to have new mattresses without Dad having to fork over his hard-earned cash. Because our big garden provided vegetables and the mountain provided venison, we never lacked for food. But when it came to warm bedding, mattresses, clothing and other necessities, Dad had to come up with the money.

Mom decided that we were going to put in the necessary time to earn our mattresses as soon as the project started. Until school was out for Dora and me, Mom was the only one who could start the program.

Work was nothing new to us. We were accustomed to working hard for everything we had. Leola had been helping Mom cook for quite some time and, with Effie's help, she also kept an eye on the twins. I would be seventeen in March, and Dora would turn fourteen in May. We were old enough to handle this new venture as just a different type of work. However, we didn't realize how much time it would take to earn one mattress, let alone the four that Mom said we needed. We would have to work many weeks.

The project got under way in early March. Men and women spent as many days as they could on the project. The men's hours were limited to the time they could spare from their spring farmwork. By the time school was out for us, the adults had completed several mattresses.

On our first day of work a the grange hall, we noticed the well-run system that had been set up, with mattresses in various stages of completion. While some of the long tables provided ample work space, others were stacked with bales of cotton, rolls of sturdy blue-and-white striped ticking, spools of heavy thread, several long-handled flat wooden paddles resembling oars, and piles of loose cotton batts. Two women had brought their treadle sewing machines from their homes.

Dessie had assigned workers their jobs, along with instructions, and handed out work assignments to the new arrivals. She led us to some long tables where a handful of people were pounding firm layers of white cotton which would eventually be stuffed into the ticking. We picked up our paddles and started whaling away. At first it seemed an easy task, but in twenty minutes my arm was as tired as if I'd been mixing a cake, beating it by hand. I kept beating, although my arm soon felt like it was ready to drop off. Dora wasn't as strong as I, but she hadn't yet stopped to rest. I shouldn't have been surprised — she always was a plucky kid.

Finally, Hazel's mother told me my cotton was fluffy enough. Thankful to be able to rest, I carried it over to the assembly table, where Mom and two of our other neighbors were layering the fluffy cotton into the ticking.

By the time I brought another batt to my table to prepare, I'd had a chance to look around at all the busy workers. Some were measuring ticking fabric; others were forming and hand-sewing the edges of a mattress. "Grandma" McKern was sewing strips of the ticking together, and Pady Rose was working at a sewing machine. Some were hand-stitching the big gap through which the last of our fluffy cotton had been stuffed, while Dessie was going from one table to another, lending a hand. Even "Grampa" McKern, who had only one arm, was doing his share of the work.

When the summer weather arrived, the hall became hot and stuffy and made pounding the cotton a disagreeable task. The stifling, still air — thick with lint around the pounding tables — made it worse. Following our paddles in their steady up-and-down rhythm, tiny wisps of cotton floated around our faces until we were almost afraid to breathe.

Even though all the windows were wide open, there wasn't a breeze to blow the lint away or to cool down the room. Even after our arms got used to beating cotton to the fluffy stage, our paddles felt like lead weights. We rested occasionally, but it became a matter of pride to keep going as long as we possibly could. We were glad when the lunch hour gave us a much-needed break, and we escaped into the outdoors. While we sat in the shade of the trees and ate our sandwiches, we breathed deeply, sucking fresh air into our lungs.

At one time or another, almost every family in the area had worked in the mattress project. To earn a low-cost mattress, women let their housework go, and men shorted their time spent on farmwork to put in the required hours. The project Dessie McCarroll had started working on in March was finished late in the summer. We were grateful for several reasons: we all had new mattresses that had cost us little or no money. We had done all the work ourselves and, lastly, the hard work was finally over.

❧ ❧

In 1988, Ethel Holter wrote to me about the grange project and said she still had her mattress. Saying Paul had worked several days, she sent me a quote from his journal, dated March 26, 1941, which read, "Ethel went to the hall to make mattresses. I finished plowing the field south of the barn and went down at noon. Don't care much for mattress making."

Letha Peters commented on it, too: "Dee McKern and Tom [Peters] were the only ones who knew how and could sew the edges to make the roll around the top."

In the years after I left home, I went back for visits as often as I could. I'd look at these mattresses that we had made and marvel that they were still in good shape. Mom used them the rest of her life.

51

Leola's Apple Pie

Threshing time came when Mom, Dora and I were still working at the grange hall. With our grain bundles already hauled in from the fields and stacked in a convenient spot for the thresher, Dad didn't need as large a threshing crew as usual. But even the few men had to be fed, and Mom didn't want to miss any time in "working out" our free mattresses.

After much cogitation, she put ten-year-old Leola in charge of cooking the noon meal and taking care of the little girls. We three would be home in time to fix a big supper for the men. Mom left Leola with instructions to open several quarts of canned venison, use canned corn and green beans, and make the gravy. For dessert, Mom told her to open a half-gallon jar of peaches. Effie and the twins could set the table and keep the woodbox filled.

Leola set to work long before it was time for dinner and found herself with extra time on her hands. As she surveyed the menu, she decided that an apple pie would be a lot more welcome than canned peaches.

The girls went to the orchard and picked a few of the ripest green apples, keeping an eye on the twins. There was enough dry pie mixture left from the week before and, with the help of Effie, who peeled the apples, Leola got to work. She had measured out the amount of sugar she would need for the filling and soon had assembled the pie. She finished with a sprinkling of cinnamon over the sliced apples, and the crust folded snugly over the top. Then she put the pie into the oven to bake.

A few minutes later, Leola spotted her measured bowl of sugar, which she had forgotten to use. She was in a quandary as to what to do. Later she told Mom that she had even considered removing the pie from the oven, peeling the top back and adding the sugar, but it was too late for that. She decided to just tell the men to add sugar to their dessert.

Dad and the crew arrived for dinner right at noon, and within minutes Leola had steaming plates of food in front of the hungry men. She served the pie for dessert, and when Dad took his first bite, he looked up, said not a word but reached for the sugar bowl, poured several heaping spoonfuls of sugar on top of his pie, and quietly passed the bowl on to the men. No one man puckered up at the first bite of the tart pie, but piled on the sugar and kept a straight face while telling Leola how delicious the flaky crust and the juicy apples were. They all appreciated the young girl's efforts and were kind enough not to tease her about baking a sugarless pie.

↪ ↩

True to her early training, Leola turned out to be a first-rate cook. She makes delicious apple pies and remembers to add sugar. Not long ago she said, "For years afterward, whenever he saw me, Verlie Pitts [one of the crew] inquired how my pie-baking was coming along. We laughed good-naturedly, remembering that tart apple pie of long ago."

52

Fun at
Quillisascut Grange

There was always anticipation in the air when we were going to a dance! Getting ready for the dance didn't take much time. After our baths, we smoothed Pond's cold cream on our faces and patted a little bit of loose powder over it. Mom used a light shade, but for my sun-tanned skin I liked Rachele. The way Mom said "Rashell" made it seem fancy and sophisticated. Mom and I put on red lipstick. Dora, only thirteen, used Tangee. (Tangee natural lipstick, orange in its hard, waxy form in the tube, turned pink when applied. I had used it until I was fourteen, when Mom let me use a brighter lipstick.)

At one time, a young married couple was staying with us until the man could find a job. His wife taught us how to make mascara. We hadn't known anyone could *make* mascara, so we watched with interest as Alice took a small dab of soot off the underside of a stove lid and mixed it with a tiny bit of melted lard. Using the flat side of a toothpick, she put some of the sooty black mixture on her blonde eyelashes. It made them look so long and thick, we had to put some on our lashes. My final touch was to put a dab of Evening in Paris cologne behind my ears.

The mascara was great — especially since it hadn't cost anything. The raw materials were always available, and we could make up a small amount whenever we needed it. (We used our home-made mascara for a couple of years before we broke down and spent money to buy Maybelline.)

After supper, all ten of us had taken a turn in the tub. Saturday night was bath night, as well as dance night. But we bathed on Friday night if we were going to go to Colville on Saturday. Mom wouldn't let us go to town dirty.

Our bathtub was a round galvanized washtub, and our bath "room" was a space in the kitchen near the cookstove. On cold days we were glad to bathe and dress in a warm spot. Heating a boiler full of water on the stove took at least half an hour and required a good, hot fire. All these preparations were lot of work. We brought in the oval-ended copper-bottomed wash boiler that hung on the outside wall near the kitchen door and set it on the stove. It required several buckets of water to fill it. We placed the boiler's fitted lid on to make it heat faster, while we kept a hot fire going.

When the water was ready, we poured some into the washtub, then added more cold water to the boiler to heat for the next person's bath. Baths for ten people required a lot of hot water and took a great deal of time. Our washtub didn't have much room in it for tall people. With my long legs, I sat with my knees pulled up almost to my chin. There was just enough room left in the tub for me to swish the washcloth around in the water and wash. We washed each other's backs — Mom did mine, and I did hers.

It took two sets of hands to empty the heavy tub of bathwater. Each person grabbed a handle and carried the tub to the door, then dumped the water into the ditch. The process went on for each bath: the next bather filled the tub, then emptied it. The last one to take a bath washed out the tub and hung it and the boiler back up on their nails on the outside wall.

Dad and Joe didn't take much time getting ready. They only had to shave, bathe, and get dressed. They didn't have to fuss with long hair and make it curly like we did.

Finally, everyone was ready to go. We crowded into the Nash, squeezing in next to each other, with the little girls perched on our laps. We knew we were going to have a good time at the dance, so we didn't mind being crowded during the short ride to the grange hall.

❦ ❦

Years later, when a Japanese friend soaped my back in a public bath in Japan, I thought of our family's Saturday-night baths in the old galvanized washtub. As I rubbed the bar of soap over Mrs. Numijiri's back, I could almost feel my mother's firm shoulders under my hand.

In an antique store recently, I spotted a well-remembered blue perfume bottle for sale. When I unscrewed the cap, that familiar scent of Evening in Paris wafted out of it. Inhaling, I had visions of dabbing some of the fragrance behind my ears and heading to the dance!

❦ ❦

"All join hands and circle to the left; allemande left and grand right and left; meet your partner with an elbow gee and an elbow haw," was the way Tom Peters started some of our square dances at the grange hall. He called lots of different dances, so we never knew what it was going to be until he started. Even after we recognized the dance, we had to listen carefully. He liked to throw in a few changes now and then just to keep us on our toes.

It didn't matter to me which ones Tom called or how he started them, just so I got to dance. The shortage of boys resulted in a few girls sitting out. I hated it when I didn't have a partner for one of the square dances and sat on a bench along the wall wishing I were dancing.

During the monthly grange meeting, the men sat on one side of the hall and the women on the other. This custom carried over to the dances without anyone giving it any thought. About the only women who sat on the men's side were visitors.

Parents took their children with them to grange meetings as well as to the dances. Mothers put babies and small children to bed in a large, double-decker homemade crib. Attached to the stage at its narrow end, the crib's six-foot length butted against the wall to one side of the stage. A railing around both levels kept the babies from rolling out.

Usually three or four blanket-wrapped babies snuggled close together while the music played and the dancers circled the floor. The music lulled them into slumber and kept them peacefully asleep throughout the evening.

While a grange meeting was in session, all children under the age of fourteen had to stay in the kitchen. When the meeting was over, we could go out into the main hall — that's when the fun began!

A few grange members furnished the music. Our grade-school teacher, Lawrence Hays, played the violin; Ethel Rupert played the piano; and her son, Warren, played the drums. Lawrence seemed to get as much fun out of playing *Turkey in the Straw* and other fast pieces as we did dancing to the beat. Unlike the Saturday-night dances, we didn't have to pay anything at these sessions after grange meetings.

Mom taught me to dance when I was ten years old, when she led me out to the dance floor and put her right arm around me. She said, "I'll show you how to do the waltz first, since it's the easiest.

Step with your right foot, slide with the left, and step with the right. That's all there is to it: step, slide, step."

After I learned the waltz, Mom showed me how to do the two-step, which I liked even better, because it was faster, and there was more turning and twirling. Mom taught Lester how to dance as well, but he didn't get as much pleasure out of it as I did. Soon Dora wanted to learn the dance steps, and Mom and I showed her how to slide her feet together. It was wonderful to keep time with the music and to turn and twirl, dancing counter-clockwise around the hall, keeping up with the grown-ups.

A year or two later, Leroy Small became one of my favorite dance partners when I discovered he liked the fast dances as much as I did. We often danced together, getting almost dizzy with all the fast whirling.

There weren't enough boys interested in dancing, so we girls danced together when we didn't have a boy partner. Dancing wasn't the only fun we had at grange. After each meeting, the lecturer arranged a short program as a bit of entertainment, which varied from question-and-answer games to recitations. During one of the programs, Patience "Pady" Abernathy Rose recited all seventeen verses of *The Highwayman,* by Alfred Noyes. Her voice held me spellbound when she got to, *"When the road is a ribbon of moonlight over the purple moor, A highwayman comes riding, riding, riding; A highwayman comes riding up to the old inn door."*

Being able to memorize such a long and complicated piece impressed me. In grade school, Mrs. Graham had assigned many poems for us to memorize, but none as long as *The Highwayman.*

Listening to Pady's recitation reminded me of her soft laugh I'd heard a few years earlier at her shivaree. Soon after she and Albert Rose were married in June of 1934, our family joined thirty or so friends and neighbors to serenade the newlyweds with a noisy welcome. Everyone gathered at dusk outside their square, two-story house and, ringing cowbells and beating on old pots, pans and washtubs, created a heck of a ruckus. One man even discharged his shotgun into the night sky.

Albert and Pady let the racket go on for several minutes before they appeared in the doorway of their home, and greeted their friends. When Dad's turn came, he was laughing his big laugh as he grabbed Albert's hand and pumped it saying, "I hope your first one's a boy!"

I was embarrassed by his remark, because at ten years of age I'd heard what caused babies. I thought Pady was a little embarrassed, too. But Albert grinned, and it was then that I heard Pady's soft laugh.

❧   ❧

A letter from Pady in 1992 recalls that evening: "At the shivaree we served homemade candy — gobs of it — fudge and divinity that my sister, Rose, and I made."

❧   ❧

During a grange meeting when I was sixteen, Ina McKern, the lecturer, announced that the state grange was sponsoring a writing contest. The subject was "Safety on the Farm," and anyone under eighteen could enter. We would have to turn our essays in at the next meeting so that Ina could send them to the state grange for judging.

A few of us decided to enter the contest. I thought about it a lot, but I couldn't think of much to say, so my essay wasn't long. About a month later, Ina announced that in our grange Betty-Jo Peters had won first place and I had won second. As part of her program, she asked us to read our essays to the group. It made me feel special, and I was sure Betty-Jo was pleased as well.

After I joined the grange, I decided that attending meetings was more fun than staying in the kitchen. Mom was chaplain, and I was proud when I was elected to office, as Ceres, one of the three Graces. It was my job to carry the flag before we recited the *Pledge of Allegiance* and then return it to its stand.

About once a month, the grange hired a small band and sponsored dances on Saturday nights, charging a dollar admission per couple. The music started at nine in the evening and ended at one in the morning. At eleven o'clock, the band took a thirty-minute break, and everyone went to the kitchen, where the grange ladies had sandwiches, coffee and dessert ready.

By the time Dora and I had become teenagers, we could follow the lead of any boy on the dance floor. The only times I was embarrassed for missing a step was when Toar Lickfold added an unexpected routine to the middle of his two-step. I could never guess when it was coming. But I enjoyed dancing with him and was glad when he asked me. Ever since he'd walked to school with us when I was six, I had looked on him as an older brother.

At a dance in the fall of 1938 (I had just graduated from the eighth grade), I was surprised when Lawrence Hays, who had been my teacher for the last two years, asked me to dance for the first time. He told me it wasn't proper for him to dance with his pupils, but since I was now in high school, he could do so. He also told me to call him "Lawrence" instead of Mr. Hays. From then on, I could count on him dancing with me at least once during the evening.

Lawrence's wife, Ruby Lickfold Hays, became my first grown-up friend. She listened to whatever I said as if it were really important. Mom and Dad *had* to like me and listen to my stories, but Ruby wasn't related to me and liked me anyway! Much like her brother, Everett (Toar), she laughed easily and had a good time whatever she did.

The Saturday-night dances lasted longer and were more fun than the casual dance sessions after grange meetings. Often as many as a hundred people came to the event — some came from as far away as Kettle Falls and Colville. Whenever they found someone who could borrow his father's car, a few of my high school classmates from Kettle would arrive at the dance together.

Not many high school boys took dates to the dances. The young men didn't own cars, and in most cases wouldn't have had the money to buy gas or pay the admission charge for their dates. Almost all the young people went to the dances with their parents and danced with everyone, rather than having their own dates.

When the music started, the girls waited on their side of the hall for someone to ask them to dance. The men either sat on the other side of the big hall or clustered at the end of the hall near the door. As they made their way to our side, I hoped one of them would stop in front of me to ask: "May I have this dance?"

It wasn't often that kids from Kettle came to our dances at Pleasant Valley, but one time during my senior year, several of them arrived together. When the band started playing *Oh Johnny, Oh Johnny,* I jumped up from the bench as classmate John Hardwick stopped in front of me and uttered those magic words. It was a fast piece, and we laughed and had a good time as we circled the floor, spinning and swooping to the music while singing, "Oh Johnny, oh Johnny, how you can love!"

Toar danced the next dance with me. I'd known Toar most of my life — ever since I was a five- year old waving goodbye to him and Lester as they walked to school each morning. Anyone for miles around knew and liked Toar. He'd grown up to be a big, handsome guy with wavy blond hair and a good personality. He had a hearty, rollicking laugh that made everyone happy just to hear it.

While the men and boys often went outside the hall to take a drink out of their bottles, we had to stay inside. Dad and Mom had a strict rule. We were *not* to go outside; only girls who didn't care about their reputations left the hall to drink or neck.

At almost all the dances, the last song the band played was *Home, Sweet Home*, and the men would head for their wives or dates. Since it was such a tradition for Dad to have the last dance with Mom, I was surprised one night when he asked me to dance. Mom had noticed that I sat out several dances and she wanted me to have her dance so I wouldn't feel left out. It was a loving, touching gesture I'll always remember.

The Saturday-night dances were simple fun, and we all looked forward to the event all week long. Driving home, Dad sang a few lines from one song or another. Sometimes it was "Show me the way to go home," but it most often was, "Be it ever so humble, there's no place like home." We felt secure and safe. Sometimes all six of us girls would fall asleep before we got home.

⋙ ⋙

Even now, many years later, whenever I happen to hear the words of those songs, I see myself again in the back seat of our car with my sisters, going home from a dance.

⋙ ⋙

Quillisascut Grange was important to most of the people who lived in Pleasant Valley, Rice, Arzina, Daisy and Gifford; it was the focal point for socializing. With few choices for entertainment in our isolated community, attending the meetings was a social event. The grange provided fun and entertainment, and a few years earlier had become the place for the Pleasant Valley School to hold its Christmas program. It also provided information to the farmers about farming: from growing crops and taking care of livestock, to homemaking, canning and sewing. One of the grange officers kept in touch with the Stevens County extension agent, passing on information as it became available. Grange members were also able to buy insurance at lower rates.

The grange hall gave farmers a place where they could hear local news, talk over their problems, and arrange for trading work. Without telephones, this was the easiest way to plan ahead and stay in touch.

Later on, Mom enjoyed the Rhododendron Club, made up primarily of grange women. The home extension agent organized the club and offered written instructions for various self-help projects. Mom took part in the craft projects, sewing contests and quilting bees. She loved making wall decorations from tin cans. Following the illustrated instructions, she used tin snips and cut flattened gold and silver tin cans into various lengths and shapes, curling the tapered ends of some of them. By joining the pieces together in layers, she fashioned several beautiful large tin flowers which looked pretty on the walls of our home.

She entered the dresses she made for us in the sewing contests and killed two birds with one stone. She learned new sewing techniques from the judging of every item — and made a dress for one of us girls.

Making friendship quilts was another sewing project. Each woman made several quilt blocks with her name embroidered on them, which she exchanged with others. When Mom had all the blocks sewn together, she had her own special friendship quilt. Several years later, the club discontinued its work projects and became more of a social club for pinochle card parties.

While our family enjoyed all the activities at the grange hall, I liked the dances best. I always felt a thrill and excitement rush in on me when Tom Peters called, "Grab your partner for a square dance!"

53

Pleasant Valley Boys Go to War

Riding the bus to school on December 8, 1941, we heard the shocking news which eddied from seat to seat like a whirlwind. Students who had listened to the radio the night before told the rest of us that Japanese war planes had bombed Pearl Harbor! We thought the kids were joking and had a hard time believing them. After all, we weren't at war with Japan. Why should they attack us?

The next day it came over the radio that President Franklin D. Roosevelt had declared war on Japan. In my senior class, Bill Clark, Jack Underwood, Art Baxter and others talked about going to the army recruiting station to enlist. Graduation was six months away, and the boys eager to serve their country didn't want to wait that long to fight back. In Pleasant Valley, first one young man then another, went off to war. Toar Lickfold, Ernie and Ab McKinney were among the first to go.

Until the war was over, no one knew exactly where their loved ones were fighting. Toar saw raging battles in several smaller islands in the South Pacific. Ernie was on the Bataan Peninsula when the Japanese invaded the Philippines and was captured on Bataan along with thousands of other young American soldiers. He survived the infamous Bataan Death March, where countless men lost their lives.

Ernie lived through near-starvation and torture during his subsequent imprisonment in Capas, Tarlac and Santo Tomas in Manila. Later, he was taken to Japan in a ship's hold and subjected to unspeakable inhuman treatment during three years of forced labor in the mines of Japan.

Mick Johnson, who grew up on a farm near Rice, worked on Wake Island in April of 1941 for a naval contractor. In December, before the company could finish its work, Japanese attacked Wake Island and made prisoners out of everyone left alive. Wounded during the invasion, Mick was among the first Americans captured. He spent the next four years in prison camps in Japan and in parts of Japanese-occupied China. Until 1943, his parents didn't know whether he was alive or dead. He was released from a prisoner-of-war camp in 1945. Mick's older brother, Charles, an army officer, also served in the South Pacific.

Lester, being younger, didn't follow them to the jungles until 1943. When he learned his draft number would soon be called, he quit his job to spend a few days at home. After basic training, he was assigned to the Combat Engineers Division and sent to the Philippines. He participated in the initial landing assaults on Ulithi and Pelelieu, where savage fighting took many American lives. These smaller islands didn't make headlines like Guadalcanal and Iwo Jima, but their names earned respect for the men who fought there.

Finally, the war was over and our boys came home. Their days of deer hunting in rugged mountains, the hard work on the family farm, and the rigors of sustaining life during the Depression, had toughened them for life and and helped them survive the brutal hardships of war.

Although happy to be back, Lester, Toar and Ernie acted jittery, not quite believing they were home safe. They didn't want to talk about their war experiences. They acted as if silence would blot out the hell they had seen, and talking would bring it all back to life. They carried their invisible battle scars inside, where they didn't show.

For several months after his return, Lester was plagued with jungle rot —the nasty reminders of the steaming jungle's unforgiving heat and bone-rotting humidity. After fourteen months in a war zone, his outfit had been sent to Leyte to help bulldoze roads and landing strips through the jungles. He also helped build ramps for landing boats and eventually became an instructor in the operation of heavy equipment.

Toar Lickfold wouldn't say much about his three years of fighting in the South Pacific. The only time I heard him mention anything was shortly after the war. He and two other men were sitting under a big shade tree at the Rice store after having dug a grave in the Mountain View Cemetery for Carl Rose's burial. When I asked if he was going to the funeral services, the once-rollicking, laughing Toar looked at me somberly and replied, "I was glad to do what I could for Carl, but I can't go to his funeral; I saw too many of my friends killed in the Pacific." Pausing as if seeing their faces before him, he huskily added, "I just can't go to another funeral."

The official proclamation said the war was over, but the war wasn't over for these veterans. To them, the battles raged on in their minds.

⟨⟩ ⟨⟩

And it has continued to rage. Fifty years later, Ernie's wife Pat told me he still woke up screaming from nightmares about his imprisonment.

Mick Johnson recently wrote that, as a civilian, he had received a Purple Heart and a Bronze Star. In 1981, the United States Government declared him a navy veteran. His brother, Charles, made the army his career and, after thirty-three years, he retired as a full colonel.

After their tour in the army, Ernie, Lester and Toar never returned to the Philippines. But in February of 1982, I went there with my husband, accompanying a veterans' group that had been invited to Manila to observe Philippine Liberation Day. During a private audience with President Ferdinand Marcos in Malacanang Palace, I mentioned to him that my brother had fought in Leyte. He said, "Oh that's my wife's province." And, turning to look across the room, he called to her. Imelda Marcos, in her long, green satin gown with its butterfly sleeves, glided over to us. President Marcos continued, "Meldy, this lady's brother fought in your province."

Tilting her head and looking up at me with her dark eyes, Mrs. Marcos graciously asked, "And what was his name?," her polite question implied she might have known him.

"His name is Lester Riley," I replied. "You would not have met him. He was bulldozing roads through the jungle and dodging bullets."

Our group, which included three survivors of the Bataan Death March, toured the Bataan Peninsula, following the route the prisoners had struggled along on foot. Leaders of our veterans' group placed wreaths at various places along the route, starting at the memorial plaque at Mile Zero on Bataan and ending at the impressive white marble memorial at Capas, Tarlac, the concentration camp site and the end of the forced march. In between, they placed wreaths at Mt. Samat Memorial and at mileposts along the

March, honoring our men who had been captured. I thought of Ernie, who had been penned up here. Two of the survivors tried to tell of their capture and the ensuing Death March, but with voices breaking, they were unable to finish. The third man could not even begin.

Later on Corregidor, as we continued our tour, we stood beside the army's bombed-out concrete barracks and walked inside the dark Malintla Tunnel that had sheltered the makeshift hospital and the remnants of General Wainwright's forces during the bombings. Viewing all this and imagining the cannon fire and bombs, the smoke and dust, the wounded and dying, renewed my admiration and respect for the men who had taken the wartime "tour."

Part V
1991

Epilogue

Epílogue

The car swerving into our driveway in Tennessee jolted me back to the present. The past dissolved, and the horse taking me to school disappeared. On the long drive from Mexico my childhood had played itself out, flickering on the screen of my mind like scenes from an old movie.

With a pang I remember that players from that movie, my parents, have been gone for many years. Dad died in 1970 and Mom in 1984. Yet, I have the odd feeling I could call them if only I knew their telephone number.

My country adventures ended in 1942 when I graduated from high school and left Pleasant Valley to find work. I became a city girl because that's where the jobs were. Two years later I married Hugh Conner, who had grown up in the nearby rural area of Arzina.

That marriage lasted twenty-four years and gave us two sons and a daughter.

I later married Henry, who dropped my first name —Ines — and called me by my family name, Riley. He has taken me to many faraway places, satisfying my longings to see other parts of the world. The trips have offered me glimpses of history, shown me different cultures, and given me fascinating geography lessons. Being inside the walled cities of Morocco made me feel as if I was plunked down in another century. At the pyramids of Giza, the sight of turbaned, *djellaba*-clad Arabs astride camels sharply reminded me I was a long way from my horseback trails in Pleasant Valley.

But however interesting people in faraway places are, they can never take the place of those in my childhood who became an extended family. The time spent at Quillisascut Grange Hall left many happy memories. When I recall going home from a dance, I still feel a rich contentment and hear Dad singing, "Show me the way to go home," with Mom humming along.

Of the seven Riley kids, five still live in Washington. Kit (Dora) and I are the only ones who strayed. She lives in Arizona, where she never has any snowdrifts to plow through, and I hang my hat in Tennessee. To "study geography" now, I travel by plane instead of horseback and shanks' ponies, and in the bright lights of city living, I miss hearing the coyotes howl.

White tailed bucks killed by Dad, Mom, Lester,
Dora, Ralph and Darlene Lawson and Louie Koerner.